Daring to Dream
the story of Keighley Cougars

I decided to write this book when the sale of nine players to Leeds was confirmed in July 1997. It seemed like the end of an era during which the ups and downs of the Rugby League Club in Keighley had gripped the imagination of people from all over the country - and sometimes even farther afield. The story has not yet ended, and there will undoubtedly be more twists and turns to come, which hopefully I can document in a second edition.

In researching the story, I have talked to and interviewed players, administrators - both at Keighley and RL headquarters - and supporters, and without exception, everyone has been friendly, helpful and co-operative. I should like to thank all those who helped me with ideas and information. Peter Stell and Graham Smith were generous in allowing me to use photographs, while Susan Dodd loaned a selection from her collection. Clive Harrison supplied all the player profiles and statistics, and loaned most of the pre-1990 illustrations. The Keighley News staff were extremely helpful in allowing me free use of their archives and reading room, and also loaned some photos.

I should also like to acknowledge Simon Kelner's excellent book, 'To Jerusalem and back.'

Whilst this story is principally about the Cougar era, I felt it would be remiss of me to ignore the prvious ninety years! The B.C. part of this book can be found in historical reverse, at the end of our chief plot.

Everyone who has been involved with the club - supporters, staff, administrators, players, townspeople - feel the Cougars belong to them. That is probably the best comment on the achievements at Cougar Park in the 1990s.

Brian Lund, March 1998

Published by Reflections of a Bygone Age
Keyworth, Nottingham

Printed by Adlard Print and Typesetting Services
Ruddington, Nottingham

All rights reserved. No part of this book may be reproduced or transmitted in any form or by any means, electronic or mechanical, including photocopying, recording or by any information storage and retrieval system, without permission from the publisher

ISBN 1 900138 24 7

Foreword by Phil Larder, Keighley Cougars coach 1994-96, and currently RFU coaching advisor

Of all my achievements in rugby league - taking Widnes to Wembley in 1993, coaching England to the World Cup Final in 1995, and leading the 1996 British Lions in the Southern Hemisphere - my most enjoyable time, without doubt, was spent coaching Keighley Cougars.

Friends could not understand my logic when I moved from Widnes, with their international players, to the small second division team of Keighley. But I believed that Keighley Cougars were to be the team of the future. The Board, led by visionary chairman Mick O'Neill, had transformed Keighley RLFC, a club down and almost out, to the Cougars, a theme which embraced an entire community.

Match day became an event, and with the main stadium packed with families, with women and children predominant, crowds increased tenfold, from well below five hundred to well above five thousand. The Cougars were taking off. Playing a brand of fast, open rugby league football, they won both the Second Division Championship and the Premiership in style, and in their performances against First Division Sheffield Eagles and Warrington in the mid-season Regal Trophy they suggested that, when promoted, they would be a force to be reckoned with.

But instead of the Cougars giving Rugby League a blueprint for the Millenium, they were denied promotion. Yet again the Rugby Football League had demonstrated to the British sporting public the reasons why the most exciting and entertaining team sport in the world had failed to spread outside the confines of its own heartland in one hundred years of history.

Above: The Cougar magic (photo: Peter Stell)
Front cover: Cougar Park in 1997, with Leigh the visiting team (photo: Brian Lund)
Back cover: celebrations after winning the Second Division Championship in 1995. Phil Larder is second right on the front row, along with Ian Gately, Steve Hall and Brendan Hill (photo: Peter Stell)

INTRODUCTION

The Cougar image for Keighley Rugby League club was officially launched in August 1991 in an imaginative attempt to resurrect an outfit that had sunk to the lowest reaches of the league in recent seasons. Just 17 months before this initiative, the club had suffered its worst-ever home defeat (8-70 to Ryedale-York), followed a week later by possibly its most embarrassing, a 22-29 reverse at Nottingham City, a side in such desperate straits that local amateur players had to be regularly dragged in at the last moment to make up a team. By October 1990, most of the grandstand at their Lawkholme Lane ground was unsafe, weeds were growing through the terraces, and the future of a professional rugby league club in the town was seriously in doubt. Attendances were counted in the low hundreds, and it was obvious that if nothing was done, the club might easily fold altogether.

What followed was the most ambitious bonding exercise of club and town ever attempted in British sport. At one time, the local rugby league or soccer club was the obvious focal point of a population centre: there were few forms of alternative entertainment, players were generally local born - or lived locally - and were an integral part of the community, and travel opportunities were restricted. Until the early sixties, rugby league clubs had no need to reach out to their potential audience: that support was almost automatic. The game may have been less attractive as a spectacle than it is now, but the passion and excitement were self-fulfilling for an audience who needed its diversion from lives that apparently had fewer opportunities for stimulation.

For over two decades from the early sixties, rugby league as a whole spent much of its time soul-searching as attendances gradually dropped and occasionally slumped. The game's laws were regularly tampered with, and experiments to discourage teams from retaining possession for long periods tried. These were generally retrograde steps until the introduction of the six-tackle rule. The competitive structures of the game were altered, and ongoing efforts to spread the game's appeal beyond its traditional boundaries continued. Southend Invicta, Bridgend and Mansfield Marksmen were among Keighley's more improbable opponents in the eighties.

Powerful voices within the game held that it had to expand or die, but too often the cart was put before the horse: professional clubs were set up and allowed to join the league from areas which had no amateur base or interest in the game. The search for the holy grail of big crowds in uncharted waters continues, and the spectacle of the Paris debacle in Super League is perhaps a reminder of the fallacies of that thinking.

In Keighley, however, the launch of Cougarism aimed to revive support in the game's own heartland. The premise was that Rugby League as a product could appeal to a wider audience than had previously watched - the working-class male and schoolboys - and the marketing effort was targeted towards families and schools. The Cougar logo went hand in hand, with the club and its players reaching out into the community. The signing of Joe Grima from Widnes not only gained Keighley an experienced front row forward, but provided a community manager who was a big success in the town. Joe organised the visits of players to local schools and began the reconversion of kids to rugby league. He developed initiatives with the police to give local youngsters more to do to keep them away from trouble, and worked out an awards scheme for 'Keighley top kids' which ended with holidays in the Lake District. Joe himself won a community award for his work in Keighley. So, later, did Ian Gately. The arrival of Mary Calvert as community co-ordinator increased the tempo of club-town co-operation.

Outings to international matches at Wembley became a regular feature of the scene, with as many as 23 coaches leaving the town for some games. All this raised the profile of the club and also the goodwill that people in the town felt for it. Then the club provided free tickets for schoolchildren to home matches, and later let in under-12's free to the ground when accompanied by adults.

On the field, though, it was necessary for the first team to be successful to encourage potential supporters to identify with the town team on a regular basis. In 1989-90, Keighley had finished third from bottom of the second division, with only Nottingham and Runcorn below them. The following season, the team did better, winning 12 of its 28 games, but this was not enough to prevent it being placed in Division 3 when a new structure was evolved for the 1991-2 campaign.

"The Cougar (also known as the Puma) is a big cat which lives on the continent of America. It has a piercing scream which gives them a ferocious reputation."
(Keighley programme, September 1991)

A new broom and a culture change

The late eighties had probably been the most depressing years in the club's history. Poor results, a decaying ground, near-bankruptcy, and minimal crowds all contributed to one fact: most people in Keighley couldn't have cared less about its rugby league team. Most people - but not everyone. Former player and local hero Terry Hollindrake was the catalyst who brought together the two men whose vision was to inspire the projection of Keighley onto a national stage.

Mick O'Neill was one of those two key figures in the transformation of Keighley in the early 1990s. A supporter of the team from 1948, he revived an interest that had lapsed during time he spent in Australia when he returned to West Yorkshire in the eighties. Appalled at the dreadful state to which the club had sunk, he was encouraged by Hollindrake and another ex-player, Gary Moorby, to *'do something about it.'* Initially, he sponsored key player Terry Manning in a deal that covered pay and kit. This deal provided an introduction to the board of directors, and a chance for O'Neill to see how it all worked. He wasn't particularly impressed, and was quite upset when Manning was sold to Featherstone without his approval, even though his 'investment' was returned. He was then introduced by Hollindrake and another potential director, David Bailey, to Mike Smith, a businessman who had made his money in TV programme production and promotional videos. The quartet talked about putting together a take-over bid, but ultimately it was just O'Neill and Smith whose proposals were accepted by the Keighley board, and they were elected as directors. The existing board, which had Ian Mahady as chairman, were set in their ways, cautious, and totally unprepared for the storm that was about to hit them. On his side, O'Neill was horrified at the lack of facilities and ambition to improve. There were lots of bank accounts, but hardly any money in each. When Andy Eyres was signed, the ceremony took place not in a plush boardroom with arclights in front of the assembled media, but in a freezing cold spot under the main stand. When the idea to put on ladies' champagne nights and corporate dinners was suggested, they first had to get a kitchen. One director resigned over the expense, a hint of what might be to come. O'Neill, though, realised that potential sponsors had to be wooed in order to attract money to revive the club.

Mick O'Neill

Mike Smith, a local lad who began watching the side in the mid-1950's, had already had one brief stint as a director in 1986, but found the the experience totally frustrating. *"The existing directors had no concept of what to do to move the club forward"* he remembers. The final straw for him was when the then coach, Peter Roe, with whose ideas he empathised, resigned. Smith left as well. But he was determined to put the concepts he was formulating about how to rejuvenate the club into practice as he watched with increasing dismay the disintegration of the Lawkholme Lane ground. The introduction to O'Neill got things going.

Smith was convinced that the club needed a complete culture change; the old club, its credibility in tatters, needed its image consigning to the dustbin. Part of his ideas were wrapped up in a wider vision for the game: changing social values meant that women were now far more influential in decisions about household spending and family leisure planning, and they had to be brought into the rugby league equation. The first crucial step in the establishment of the new image was to be the renaming of the team.

Mike Smith

1991-92: The Beginning

The Cougar name, suggested by a local schoolboy in a competition to find a memorable team title, was officially launched at an August 1991 meeting at the Victoria Hall, Keighley, which included a persuasive video presentation that became one of Mike Smith's trademarks. *Cougars* was felt to be the most marketable of the various animal names put forward, and it had an alliterative quality as well.

At the start of season 1991-2, Keighley were rated at 12-1 to take the third division title; Doncaster were favourites. Despite a pre-season 54-8 thrashing by Featherstone in a friendly, enthusiasm was high for the first-ever game as Cougars. Unfortunately, the side performed poorly at Bramley, losing 12-41. *"After the hype - tripe,"* moaned the *Keighley News. "The worst possible result we could have had,"* said director Mick O'Neill. Coach Tony Fisher paid the price during the week for the result - he was unceremoniously sacked. Fisher had been appointed in July 1990, and, on the advice of certain directors, had spent the summer dispensing with the services of some players whose attitude was considered unsatisfactory. Now it appeared he wasn't considered up to the job of taking the team any further forward.

The programme for the first Cougar home game featured a photo of the ex-coach on page one and his name in lights on the inside front cover; the pace of events had been just too fast for the editor. He didn't seem to have been caught up in the new promotion, either: despite helpfully explaining for bemused fans what a cougar was, the programme didn't go overboard on hyperbole. The result was okay, with Chorley being overturned 52-12, but the crowd was a disappointing 800. *"The Bramley result cost us support and we have to build it back,"* commented O'Neill.

> *Team for Keighley's first home game as Cougars was Dixon; James, Race, A. Stephenson, Chick; Eyres, Godfrey; Hiley, Handford, Rose, Farrell, Fairbank, Gascoigne. Substitutes were Royle and Hall.*

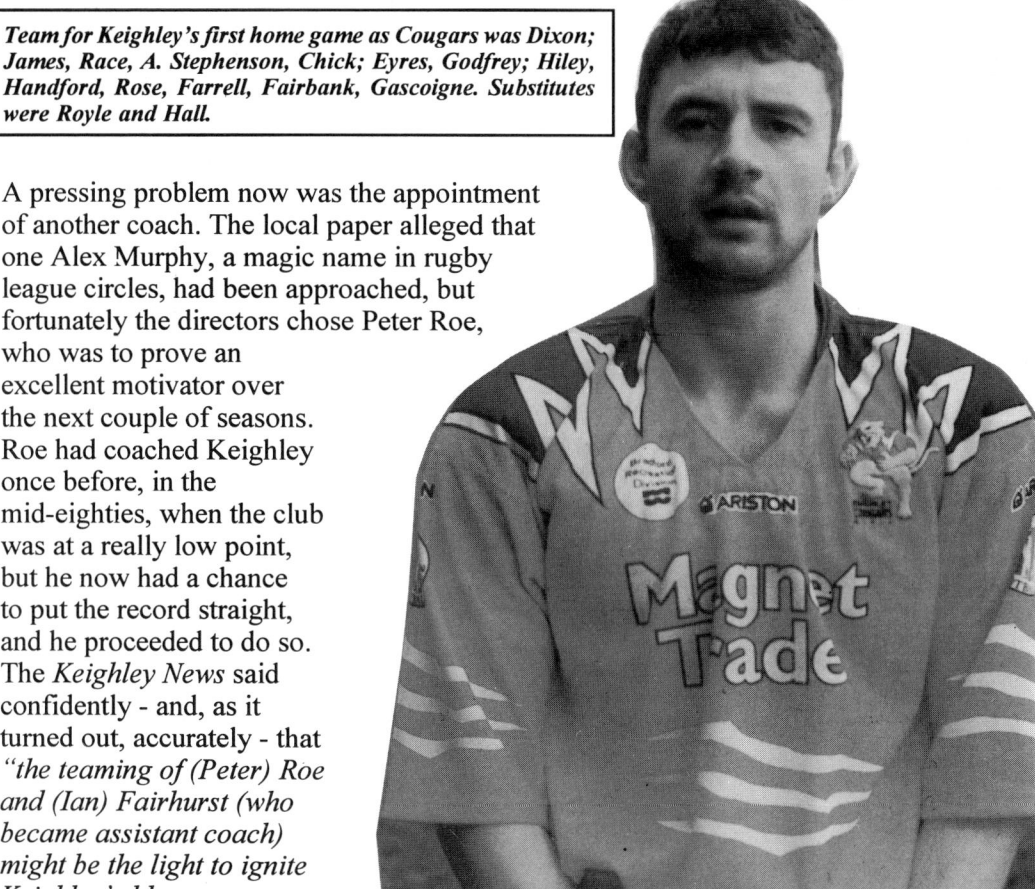

A pressing problem now was the appointment of another coach. The local paper alleged that one Alex Murphy, a magic name in rugby league circles, had been approached, but fortunately the directors chose Peter Roe, who was to prove an excellent motivator over the next couple of seasons. Roe had coached Keighley once before, in the mid-eighties, when the club was at a really low point, but he now had a chance to put the record straight, and he proceeded to do so. The *Keighley News* said confidently - and, as it turned out, accurately - that *"the teaming of (Peter) Roe and (Ian) Fairhurst (who became assistant coach) might be the light to ignite Keighley's blue touchpaper."* Meanwhile, however, the team had lost again to Bramley - in the Yorkshire Cup.

Changes were also afoot in the boardroom - Len Evans and Colin Farrar, two of the directors who'd kept the club afloat in the previous decade, were voted off the team of directors in October 1991. This was the first in a string of boardroom battles that bedevilled the club in its first few Cougar years.

Results until December were unspectacular and mixed: a draw against promotion favourites Doncaster provided some comfort, though a seaside defeat at the hands of Scarborough Pirates was a huge disappointment. Attendances remained disappointing, with only 701 watching the team beat Highfield 42-14 in early November, a game in which John Wasyliw, the ex-Halifax rugby union player, broke the club pointscoring record in a game, not for the last time. That win, and a Regal Trophy success against Hunslet the week after, prompted a eulogy from the *Keighley News: "The tide finally appears to be turning at Lawkholme Lane. Years of doubt over the club's financial future, the long drawn-out saga with the Yorkshire Co-op over the future of the ground, and safety fears over the ground appear over... Peter Roe is instilling commitment and enthusiasm"* and concluded *"a winning team is the perfect advertisement for the town."* A good display at Wigan in the Regal was followed by four successive league wins. The directors appealed to the public for more support, yet only 1,181 came to Lawkholme on December 15th to watch the Cougars beat league leaders Hunslet 40-8. Peter Roe began talking about promotion.

1992 dawned with a share issue from the Cougars, with investors being asked to buy a minimum 25 at £1 each. Chairman Ian Mahady stressed that the club was in the black, with all debts paid, and that no financial problems existed. He explained that it was costing £3,500 a week just to run the club, and that an average gate of at least 1,800 was needed to finance this - many more than the team had pulled in so far that season. The playing squad was valued at £460,000, though Peter Roe was looking to strengthen it.

Signs of the Cougar travelling support that was to be such a feature of the next few

Keith Dixon *was one of the few Keighley born players to be given a testimonial by the club. He was born on 16th September 1966 and had one season with Keighley Albion Under 17s, and a short spell with Bradford Northern Colts, before signing for Keighley on 28th August 1984, despite the interest of both Northern and Leeds. He made his full debut on 27th April 1986 against Barrow at Cougar Park, having made a substitute appearance at Runcorn on 21st April 1985, and remained at the club, apart from a three match loan spell with Hunslet, until the 1997 season when he joined Dewsbury. Keith was what is known as a 'utility' player, playing in all the back positions, originally at stand off, but latterly as a full back or winger. Whilst his versatility almost guaranteed him a first team place for most of his career, Keith was also a prolific goal kicker, occasionally grabbing valuable points with drop-goals. In his career at Keighley, Keith made a total of 264 appearances (including 27 as a substitute) and scored 95 tries, 323 goals and 21 drop-goals, giving him a total of 1,047 points for the club. He subsequently passed the century mark as far as tries are concerned when playing for Dewsbury. Keith has the dubious honour of being the only player to have played in Keighley's biggest defeat (2-92 at Leigh, 30th April 1986 and biggest victory (104-4 v. Highfield at Spotland, 23rd April 1995).*

years were evident at the next game at Doncaster, where Keighley fans were in the majority. The side struggled to edge home 14-12 in a tight game, though. The following week, a home defeat against Bramley (7-10) was watched by 1,241 - not enough for Mahady's break-even point. Money worries were eased, though, by a grant of £170,000 from Bradford Council to pay for safety work deemed necessary after the Taylor report on the state of football grounds. Two new signings raised supporters' spirits, too: Martin Wood was secured from Scarborough Pirates for a bargain £15,000 - what an investment he was to prove - and former All-Black flanker Mark Brooke-Cowden arrived, too. Cup drama followed, with three games against Barrow being necessary to see who would progress to the second round. A 7-7 draw at Barrow was followed by a 14-14 stalemate at home, before Keighley lost 0-16 in the second replay at Widnes, thereby missing out on a second round Challenge Cup game against Bradford Northern in front of the BBC TV cameras.

Keighley Cougars were now 8th in the third division out of 14 clubs, and the possibility of promotion was looking remote. A two-point win at home to Scarborough was watched by less than 1,200, and director Mike Smith urged fans to *"get behind the team."* Coach Roe lashed the players for an *"unimpressive"* display. Meanwhile, a bizarre report that ex-champion boxer Gary Mason might be the next arrival at Cougar Park began to gain credence. After increasing publicity and speculation, he eventually signed for London Crusaders instead.

Two more impressive performances followed: a 70-0 home win against a hopelessly outclassed Nottingham City, and a narrow 14-18 reverse at top-of-the-table Huddersfield, where Keighley looked every bit as good as the likely promotion team. But the season ended in an injury crisis and disappointment. A crowd of 2,100 anticipating another close game against Huddersfield was chagrined to see Keighley lose 6-30, and the following week only 742 turned up to watch Cougars beat Trafford Borough 28-14. With injuries mounting, the side scraped a one-point victory over Dewsbury before a special promotion and free ticket distribution produced a 2,000 plus crowd for the next home game against Whitehaven. This game, which Cougars won 46-24, marked the microphone debut of Mick O'Neill, whose style added significantly to the atmosphere and entertainment for the next few years. Two away defeats, one an abject 2-38 loss at Barrow, meant the team finished 7th at the end of the league season. The Premiership produced two good games against Bramley - a draw away, and a narrow win in the replay at home - but the campaign ended sadly, as an already injury-crippled Cougars were forced to play the next round at Sheffield only two days after the replay. It was Keighley's fourth match in nine days, and even coach Peter Roe had to come on as a substitute. Not surprisingly, Eagles swooped home 72-14.

Future prospects were by no means bleak, though: Magnet renewed their sponsorship agreement for the following season with another £50,000 promised injection. Their marketing director Gary Favell confirmed: *"We are showing an active interest in taking this club to the standards of the likes of Wigan."* Andy Eyres was named player of the season, and the average crowd was reported as 1,196 - an increase of 211 on the previous year. Cougars were the second biggest crowd-pullers in Division 3.

1992-93: The Breakthrough

The close season brought two crucial players to Lawkholme. First, Joe Grima came from Widnes, despite doubts about the wisdom of this from director Mike Smith. Then Ian Gately, who'd had experience with four top Australian clubs and played for Manly against Wigan in a World Club Challenge game, was signed. These two were to play a huge role in the development of the Cougars' image, and not just on the playing side. Both brought a significant physical presence (Gately was 6ft 2in and 17 stone, Grima was renowned for breaking the chairs he sat on), but also personalities ideally suited to the public relations role they were going to play. 1992-3 was going to be a serious bid for promotion season.

Gately's arrival was brokered by another ex-Manly player, Noel Cleal. Despite the massive difference in playing standard between the top Australian side and Keighley, Ian recognised that the club was ambitious and improving, and he felt the contract he'd been offered was sound. He thought that once he'd established himself in the British game, it might be possible to move to a top division club, but in the end he stayed at Keighley for

---

Peter Roe has been associated with Keighley R.L.F.C. for many years in various capacities. His first involvement was as a player when he joined his local club in 1974, making his debut on 10th March against Blackpool Borough at Lawkholme Lane. In his first spell with the club, he played 55 times, scoring 9 tries, and represented Yorkshire twice, the first time on his home ground.

From Keighley, Peter moved on to local rivals Bradford Northern, where he had a very successful career before injury brought it to a temporary end. Problems from his injury prevented him from playing for Bradford again and he returned to playing as an amateur with York before moving on to Hunslet.

In September 1985, Peter rejoined Keighley as player - coach, taking over from the ailing Geoff Peggs. In his first season back, Peter played 31 times, scoring 4 tries, but he was unable to prevent Keighley finishing the season near the foot of Division 2. The following season Peter played just 17 games, having been replaced as coach by Colin Dixon and Les Coulter. The new coaching team could not, however, improve Keighley's fortunes and the team finished the season at the very bottom of the 2nd Division.

Peter then went back to coaching, first with amateurs Keighley Albion and Dudley Hill, then with Halifax in the 2nd Division. With Halifax in the 1990/91 season, Peter guided them to promotion to the 1st Division and to the Final of the Divisional Premiership where they were narrowly beaten by Salford.

Halifax decided they needed a change of coach for the 1st Division, so the opportunity arose for Peter to return to Keighley, succeeding Tony Fisher as coach in September 1991. At last Peter was to guide his team to a trophy and, in the 1992/93 season, with the assistance of Ian Fairhurst, his team won the 3rd Division Championship, Keighley's first trophy for 90 years. Peter made his last appearance in a Keighley shirt as a substitute in the 2nd Round match of the Divisional Premiership against Sheffield Eagles at the Don Valley Stadium on 25th April 1992, when Keighley lost heavily. Having to play three games in five days was too much of a handicap against a team from a higher division.

In April 1994, Peter and Keighley parted company once again. Peter remained in coaching, taking up posts with Barrow, then Swinton.

five years and quickly became a firm favourite with the crowd: his aggressive, bullocking runs, terrific ability to offload the ball in the tackle, and appetite for making tackles, made a huge contribution to Keighley's improvement.

At the end of July 1992, the *Keighley News* announced the beginning of the second phase of Cougarmania, excitingly titled "The Breakthrough." Mike Smith claimed Keighley had its best squad for twenty years. Demand for season tickets was high, and business sponsorship was taking off. Marketing, under Smith's imaginative direction, was playing an ever-increasing part in the club's life. A pre-season friendly at home to Bradford Northern, watched by 1,042, saw Cougars win 26-16. *"The breakthrough: you better start believing,"* trumpeted the *KN*. The first league game at what was still Lawkholme Lane provided a great start to the season, with Workington Town, regarded as one of the best sides in Division 3, seen off 18-2. The local paper seemed unable to get to grips with spelling Gately's name correctly, though, providing a variety of efforts over the weeks.

> *The team that represented Keighley in that first 1992-3 game was Ball; Walker, Kerr, Hinchliffe, Wasyliw; Dixon, Eyres; Gately, Ramshaw, Grima, Hall, Brooke-Cowden, Wood. Substitutes were Farrell and Moses. What a front row! Only Keith Dixon and Andy Eyres were left from the team that had started the first home game of the previous season.*

A crowd of 1,332 was followed by a 1,480 attendance for the next home game, when Barrow were defeated 40-10, so numbers were beginning to creep up. But in between was a highly disappointing 12-28 loss at Hunslet, where disappointed Peter Roe called the handling a disgrace. *"We let a lot of people down."* There was, of course, a lot of pressure on the side to perform; the escalating publicity and hype was attracting the townsfolk back to rugby league again, but it meant that more people were noticing the results, too. Those continued to be patchy through September, with another league defeat and a Yorkshire Cup exit at the hands of Wakefield Trinity. Already, too, hints of the cash tightrope that Keighley seemed destined to tread forever: the club couldn't afford to buy Jason Ramshaw, who had been on loan from Halifax, though the asking price was only £7,500. The fact that there was no home game - and therefore no turnstile revenue - from 20th September to 1st November didn't help: another case of muddled planning from Rugby League HQ. All this was forgotten, though, on that latter date, when the new terracing on the old 'scratting shed' side of the ground was officially opened, and a major development plan launched. The ground, too, got a fresh name, Cougar Park, which Keith Reeves, who was then rugby correspondent of the *KN*, thought was *"crazy."* The newspaper continued to refer to the ground as Lawkholme Lane for a long time afterwards, somehow reluctant to throw away tradition as readily as the go-ahead directors. Lambs to the Cougar slaughter on that day were the hapless Nottingham City, who, despite being in an area apparently ideally suited for RL expansion, got no cash or encouragement from Chapeltown Road, headquarters of the Rugby League. On this sacrificial day, they were duly hammered 86-0 in front of 1,333 spectators. Good news on another front - the steady progression of the club's junior sides - was tempered by Andy Eyres requesting a transfer on the grounds that the directors had broken contract promises. Eyres was listed at £95,000 and there were no takers; he stayed at Keighley, much to the relief of supporters.

By the end of November, Cougars had moved up to fourth in the third division table after winning 16-14 at Ryedale York, and main sponsors Magnet provided another generous cash boost. A fortnight later came a depressing home defeat to Whitehaven to complete the first half of the league programme, but that third Division 3 reverse was to be the last of the season: 14 straight league wins were about to unfold. At the end of 1992, Keith Reeves was generous in his praise of the achievements at Cougar Park, despite his distaste for that name. *"The ground now looks like a sports venue instead of a derelict mass of old wood and chicken wire. The team has been transformed. Roe and his coaching staff are doing a great job with limited resources."*

1993 continued to bring good news and positive signs. The Cougar Cats ladies' team was re-formed, and beat Birkenshaw 12-0 in their first outing. A new share issue was announced to encourage a greater flow of capital, and the best crowd of the season (2,074) watched Keighley beat York 22-15. A rare defeat followed in a magnificent Challenge Cup game at Craven Park, Cougars losing out 28-30 in a thrilling finish. On 21st February, 400 female supporters turned up for a special 'ladies' day' when the Cougars entertained Chorley (and a 1,945 crowd) with a 78-6 success. A week later, John Wasyliw broke Brian Jefferson's club pointscoring record as he hit 338 for the season. On the first Saturday of March, over 1,000 supporters trekked to the Lancashire seaside,

John Wasyliw had a remarkably short career with Keighley, but it was a career which made a big impression on the record books. John had made his mark at the Halifax Rugby Union club as a consistent goal kicker, and it was mainly for that reason that Tony Fisher signed him in March 1991. John was only 23 years old when he joined Keighley, so he had a potentially long career ahead of him in Rugby League. As it was, he played just three full seasons with Keighley before retiring to a more secure career in banking. A crowd pleaser was very definitely lost to Rugby League, for, as well as being a prolific goal kicker, he was becoming a very good wing three-quarter.

He played 75 games for Keighley, and between February 1992 and September 1993 he scored in 46 consecutive matches, touching down for 37 tries and kicking 238 goals. During that period he took the records for goals and points in a season which had both previously been held by Brian Jefferson. That was in Keighley's 3rd Division Championship winning season of 1992/93 when he kicked 187 goals and scored 490 points, including a record 15 goals in the match against Nottingham City on 1st November 1992. He became, and still is, the only Keighley player to have played and scored in every game of a season. In the following season he went on to score a record setting 36 points in the match against Nottingham City on 31st October 1993.

providing Blackpool with an unexpectedly big attendance, but bringing the Cougar roar to turn an away match into almost a home one. The 82-8 victory had most people at the club now harbouring real hopes of winning Division 3, but at just this highly-charged moment, the Rugby League, with its normal impeccable timing, decided to revert to two divisions for the following season. The existing second division, with only eight clubs playing each other on four league occasions, had not proved the success Gary Hetherington of Sheffield Eagles had hoped for when he had first suggested it. So Keighley would not actually be promoted if they won their division - they would just step into a revamped Division 2 along with all the teams they'd thrashed that season. This unfortunate circumstance was to be repeated two seasons later with even more disastrous consequences.

The roles of Mike Smith and Mick O'Neill had developed into the pattern they were to follow through until 1996. While Smith worked largely behind the scenes on marketing and promotion, O'Neill was the 'front' man, conspicuous on the microphone, the public face of Cougars. Curiously, Mike Smith was the extrovert one of the two, Mick O'Neill the introvert - except when he was behind a microphone and in front of a big crowd.

Meanwhile, everything was going well on the field. Three days after a crowd of 3,450 watched Dewsbury beaten 33-24, Cougars went to the top of the division with yet another emphatic win, by 80 points to 8 at Highfield. Peter Roe was ecstatic, and gave the supporters full credit: *"The fans have inspired the team and regained their faith after years in the wilderness,"* he enthused. Hunslet were next for the Cougar Park treatment, which by now included the partisan commentary of Mick O'Neill and a special record for each player, trotted out whenever anyone scored. James Lowes, now of Bradford Bulls but on this occasion Hunslet, asked the referee *"can't you shut that guy up?"* *"Don't let 'em score any more tries, then, lad,"* suggested the official. Keighley won this one 49-8. And so to Good Friday 1993, when Batley were the visitors and Keighley could clinch the championship with a win. On what O'Neill said was the most exciting day of his time with the club - and what many supporters regard as the high point of the Cougar saga - sponsors Magnet laid on fireworks and entertainment, and Batley duly surrendered in front of a huge crowd of over 5,000. Cougarmania had taken hold at last. The premiership quest that followed fizzled out disappointingly at Rochdale, and John Wasyliw finished the season just short of two more records. He missed out on Joe Sherburn's 30 tries in a season for Keighley by just one, and his 490 points was only six adrift of Leeds' fifties superstar Lewis Jones's all-time RL record. As some compensation, his 187 goals were the most by any player in the league that season. Martin Wood, probably the most creative player in the side, won the supporters' 'Player of the season' award, and went on to get the prestigious 'Man of Steel' 3rd Division award at the RL's ceremony. On May 8th, the players paraded round Keighley in an open-top bus to a deserved enthusiastic reception.

More good news was to come, as the signings of Nick Pinkney and Greg Austin were announced. Pinkney was a tremendous prospect, and O'Neill was delighted to secure his signature for what was then a record £35,000 Keighley transfer payment: the gifted centre was to play a huge part in the next two seasons. The O'Neill signings were often inspired, and many of the players who came to Keighley at very reasonable fees proved an excellent investment. Unfortunately, though, that investment was never financially realised. Signings were financed by sponsor deals or direct appeals to supporters - when Brendan Hill was signed, O'Neill went on to the pitch to launch a £10,000 fund. And because payments were usually spread over a number of months, the necessary cash could be put together over a period. Many of the players were signed by O'Neill personally after long hours on the telephone or the road. Austin, though, was a rare mistake: he had a track record that underlined his talent but hinted at possible problems; and his signing was to prove perhaps O'Neill's worst decision, one that set the club off on yet another cash crisis. The club had incurred a loss of just over £44,000 in the previous season, and worse was to come. Coaches Peter Roe and Ian Fairhurst signed a new 2-year deal, and at the end of June 1993 details were released of the under-19 Academy side that would be set up.

Ian Gately was one of the few overseas players to have had a long term influence on the Keighley team. Born in Sydney, Australia on 21st March 1966, Ian had played with Parramatta and Manly in the Winfield Cup competition and had played for Manly in the very first World Club Challenge against Wigan in 1987 in front of 36,895 spectators. He was a strong, some may say fierce, running prop forward and had also represented the Australian President's XIII against Great Britain in 1988. Ian joined Keighley in August 1992 and his skills were put to good use in six campaigns, winning two championships and appearing in two Divisional Premiership finals. Ian was a skilled ball handler, who was so feared by opponents that occasionally ruthless means were used to bring him down. He was able to create many a try for his colleagues by releasing the ball round the back of his tacklers. His own try scoring feats were normally restricted to the good use of his power near to the line, but his 23 tries from 154 appearances also included some longer range efforts. Ian left Keighley at the end of the 1997 season, retiring back home to his own sports bar in Sydney.

John Wasyliw signs for Keighley with a delighted coach Tony Fisher and director Mike Smith

Community Cougars

Mary Calvert (photo: Keighley News)

"It was more like a spiritual experience." (Mary Calvert, talking about her first visit to Cougar Park)

Not wishing to stand still or lose the momentum of publicity, the club launched what Mike Smith called *"a major initiative to become an indelible part of town life."* It evolved originally from the 'player of the year' award, chosen by supporters. Why not begin to involve the community more in the life of the club, encourage businesses to feel part of Keighley Cougars via sponsorship schemes at varying levels? Players would be seconded to schools, and attempts were to be made to turn youngsters away from crime and drugs. This was an initiative that won fairly immediate nationwide publicity, and catapulted the town and its rugby team into the national media in a way that the actual games played by the town team could never have done. *KN* editor John Liddle proclaimed the club as *"a modern rugby league team to be proud of,"* and detected *"a town-wide buzz"* about the initiative.

The driving force behind it was Mary Calvert, who was appointed as the club's Community Co-ordinator, and who was to play the crucial role in the programme that unfolded. Mary had not really been aware of what had recently been happening at Cougar Park, though she had watched matches in the sixties and seventies. Her son, attracted to a game via a free ticket given away by Joe Grima on a visit to his school, persuaded Mary to come down to watch, and she was immediately captivated by the atmosphere. *"I couldn't believe it,"* Mary recalls, *"it wasn't like a rugby match - more a kind of spiritual experience."* At that match, a chance meeting with Mike Smith, who she knew from schooldays, resulted in a suggestion that she take on some kind of community programme for the club. Mary was delighted to have a chance to become involved. For the next three and a half years her life was dominated by Keighley Cougars and the partnership with the community. Her working week stretched to around 60 hours and totally transformed her personal life.

Mary's first task was to prepare a submission for a grant from 'Sportsmatch,' a Department of Heritage initiative which provided money for club schemes. In her presentation, Mary stressed the aims of *"raising the profile of Rugby League, both locally and nationally...developing positive contacts with schools...using the Cougar classroom to encourage enthusiasm for RL and academic achievement...developing a symbiotic relationship between Keighley Cougars and Keighley children."* She stressed the four proposed elements that would characterise the club's involvement with the community: the coaching development scheme, the involvement of children with the game, the Cougar classroom, and the community programme of targeting drug and alcohol abuse, fighting juvenile crime, and using rugby league to encourage an ethos of achievement and good behaviour. The £75,000 award that was granted by Sportsmatch was supposed to be matched by a similar sum from the club. This was eventually taken up jointly by Magnet, Cougars' main sponsors, and a Surrey-based manufacturer of electrical goods called Whirlpool. When Magnet, who placed huge orders with them, first used their economic influence to induce Whirlpool to put cash into a rugby league club in a small Yorkshire town, the Southern firm must have been somewhat bemused, but they quickly became impressed with the club, and in particular its community co-ordinator. Local MP Gary Waller, who was to become increasingly supportive of the club, also leant his influence to the Sportsmatch award negotiations.

The existing player involvement with any organisations in the town where they could be of use -particularly schools, youth clubs and hospitals - was extended. At first, the most enthusiastic exponents were Joe Grima and Andy Eyres, who would raise the profile of the club and tell children about the game. Grima became a very popular figure both at the club and in the town, and had been an inspired signing. An immensely likeable man, he worked extremely hard at his community role.

Eyres and Nick Pinkney were particularly good at going into schools on 'media days' and helping with projects, while some players also assisted the local police 'summer scheme.' Ian Gately and Gareth Cochrane, too, proved great ambassadors, but the most outstanding player influence was that of Grant Doorey, an Australian who was also a trained teacher. Grant was instrumental in persuading schools to take up rugby league as part of their sports curriculum: from only two that were playing the game at the start of 1993, the figure mushroomed to 34 four years later, with regular annual inter-schools competition days becoming an established feature. The encouragement of these schools into introducing or extending rugby league involved players taking regular coaching sessions to support teacher activity, and it worked extremely well. By the autumn of 1993, Joe Grima was planning to take 1,000 local schoolchildren to Wembley for the forthcoming test against New Zealand, another idea which was to be repeated for the following three autumns. Other involvements included fun things like zany T-shirts and 'snap a Cougar' contests, devised to involve as many people as possible. The whole groundbreaking scheme, though, won the support of the local paper, the police, politicians, and business, including Royal Mail. By the middle of June, the *KN* reported, perhaps exaggerating slightly, that *"the world has gone Cougar crazy!"* After eight months, Joe Grima won a local business award (a cut-glass bowl) for 'Employee of the year' to mark his community work. Two months later, though, he left this side of his job with Cougars to join local firm Raiseprint as a rep.

Perhaps the most enterprising idea was the 'Cougar classroom,' set up in November 1993, and based on the 'classroom on the park' at Sunderland Football Club's Roker Park ground. Financed by the Training and Enterprise Council, a 'classroom' was set up in the Bronte Bar at the ground where lessons based on the rugby club and the way it was run could be organised, using disciplines involved in the national curriculum, while investigating how the club was run in a commercial sense. A local teacher, Barry Shinn, was seconded for a year to run the scheme, and he was assisted by player Kevin Marr - and when Kevin returned to Australia, by Nick Pinkney. 30 children at a time came to Cougar Park for the day to work: maths, English, geography, science, design and technology, personal and social education were incorporated into a series of tasks that involved things like measuring the stand, investigating supporters' routes to the ground on matchdays, working out hypothetical gate receipts, writing reports on games, learning about players' diets, and so on. Children as young as four, and students up to the age of 19, were involved. After a year, funding was taken over by a drugs education organisation, and the emphasis changed to a 'healthy living' syllabus. The 'Cougar classroom' had several spin-offs. It came to be seen as a place which could help severely disadvantaged or disabled children, whose involvement with a group on an activity as basic as passing a rugby ball around could bring more out of them. The schoolboys and girls who came to the classroom - 5,000 of them in three years - took away a sense of belonging to the club which spread throughout the community, and translated itself in increased attendances and the phenomenon of 'family supporters.' Kids who'd been down would bring along parents and siblings to matches, allowing more people to sample the Cougar experience. The club came to be viewed as a kind of 'guru' in this pioneering type of community education, and other rugby league club's representatives came along to see how it all worked. Mary Calvert was on the verge of seeing

Joe Grima gets stuck in at Woodville Horticultural Training Centre (photo: Mary Calvert)

Publicity shot for a competition to win a washing machine as part of the Whirlpool-Magnet Foundation. Mary Calvert joins players Gareth Cochrane, Andy Eyres, Ian Gately and Nick Pinkney (photo: Keighley News)

Cougar kids at Wembley on one of the grand outings (photo: Mary Calvert)

similar schemes set up at other clubs by the time she eventually left the Cougars set-up: of professional rugby league clubs, Warrington and Bradford Bulls have since instituted similar schemes, but the influence of the Cougars' innovative ideas have spread far beyond the sport's boundaries.

The 'Cougar classroom' generated a good deal of TV, radio and press coverage, and the club received much outside help - decorating and photography from Keighley College, design and artwork from the Jackson partnership, stationery from the National and Provincial Building Society. In the summer of 1994, Barry and Nick visited lots of schools in the Bingley, Shipley and Wharfedale areas to spread the gospel.

Schools in Keighley were delighted with the involvement of the club. *"All it took to fire the enthusiasm of students and staff here at Branshaw School was a visit from Grant Doorey and the offer of a chance to work with members of the Keighley Cougar team,"* wrote the school's head teacher. *"It is good to see a high profile, successful club such as the Cougars so keen to develop links with local schools,"* commented Greenhead Grammar School. Players went to schools to give the PAWE's (Personal Awards for Excellence) to children who'd earned them. *"Your Cougar Park classroom is being used by some of our more problematic students in an effort to motivate them and make their attitudes more positive,"* said head teacher John Roberts from Oakbank School. *"I express my appreciation. I hope very much that you will be able to continue with this kind of educational and community support."* Particularly impressed was Woodville Horticultural Training Centre: *"The regular visits by players to Woodville means an awful lot to the trainees here,"* wrote Senior Training Officer Jo Lees, *"The commitment you have shown to the Keighley community and especially our trainees is reflected by the staunch support and loyalty that everyone here feels towards the club. The Cougars continue to prove themselves an integral part of Keighley by investing time and energies into projects for disadvantaged groups."*

Mary Calvert herself took on a time-consuming role, both at the ground and outside it, regularly talking to young children and teenagers on social and drug-related issues. She increasingly came to believe that the rugby club could provide a focus for the town which had seen its community change radically in the previous two decades. To understand the phenomenon of Cougarmania, it is important to place it in the context of Keighley's development. Until the sixties, most employment in the town had been provided by textile mills and big engineering firms, with social clubs, sports facilities and large workforces giving people a sense of identity, belonging and self-worth. With the gradual closure of many of these firms and their partial replacement by smaller service industries, that sense of identity disappeared, and Keighley at times had the appearance of a dying town. The rugby club had struggled for much of the late seventies and early eighties, with attendances dipping to a few hundred, and there seemed to be nothing which could unite the community. When the rugby club was re-invented as the Cougars in 1991, there was at last something which could actually give the town a focus again. Folk were presented with something to which they could feel they belonged, something which again gave them a sense of identity. The stunning successes on the field of the team between 1992 and 1995 put the town in the rugby headlines, while the community activities ensured Keighley a national (and, at times, international) stage. The club became an inspiration. *"It is no exaggeration,"* Mary went on record as saying, *"that we were regarded as trailblazers. We have created something which can not only be used by other sporting organisations, but can be transferred to any high-profile commercial enterprise. We have shown through our work that we can help tackle the problem of drugs misuse."*

Though Mary Calvert, Grant Doorey, and some of the teachers who got involved in the Cougar programme at the ground and in the community were passionately convinced of its value, not everyone at the club regarded it in quite the same light. The club directors tended to have cashflow and playing success as their two priorities, and were apt to view things like the 'Cougar classroom' as a distraction - though they enjoyed the excellent public relations that community activities brought in. They were more interested about pouring money into players than club administration. What they often failed to appreciate was that the positive p.r. could attract sponsorship, and that the massive goodwill generated was bound to be reflected in increased attendances and gate revenue. Some of the players were happy to become involved in the schools visiting and the classroom, but others were reluctant. Oddly, this became more noticeable when most of the playing staff went full-time, even though players' contracts normally specified involvement in the community side of the club. For those at the sharp end of the community concept, though, there was a tangibly great atmosphere, the constant feeling that the club was on the verge of something spectacular - and not just on the playing side. The belief that the club had a crucial role to play in the well-being of the town at times became almost messianic. Perhaps Cougarmania really could cure all society's ills. Perhaps kids could be led away from taking potentially destructive options through their involvement.

Local MP Gary Waller was hugely enthusiastic about all these developments: *"I've been increasingly impressed by the successful efforts of the club to develop links with the community... it's not surprising that better known top clubs have beaten a path to Keighley's door."*

Certainly, the involvement of players with role model status can have a highly positive influence on the behaviour of youngsters. When Manchester United soccer star Eric Cantona had to do community service as a punishment for his attack on a spectator, his influence was apparently startling. *"Police, probation officers, social workers and parents of the youngsters coached by the saintly Eric are convinced the 'Cantona effect' has dramatically reduced juvenile crime in what was one of the toughest areas of Greater Manchester,"* wrote Barry Hugill in *The Observer*. The force for good that Cougars players working in the community could generate was frequently underlined locally.

A huge number of folk contributed to the smooth running of the playing side, too, especially on matchdays, and the band of stewards, programme sellers, bingo ticket vendors, turnstile operators and so on could be proud of the part they were playing, of the stake they had in the Cougars. If they didn't always feel valued by the club's administration, they could at least bask in the reflected glory of the team. What was patently obvious, though, was the way that the supporters were absolutely passionate about their side.

Four decades ago, when the club was attracting crowds of four to five thousand, a similar figure to that which would be achieved at the height of Cougars' success in 1994 and 1995, there was not the same feeling in the town about the club. Most spectators were people who were rugby league enthusiasts. A lot of people in the mid-1990's went to watch partly because they felt that the Cougars belonged to them and to Keighley. The club had been so successful in integrating with and imposing its image on the town that it became difficult at one stage to tell which needed the other most.

The initiative appeared to have hugely positive results. Less than a year after its inception, incoming *Keighley News* editor Malcolm Hoddy was able to make his first front-page lead the story that Keighley had the lowest crime rate in the county. Juvenile crime had dropped in the past year by 13% when it was rising virtually everywhere else in West Yorkshire. Down to the Cougar Community Partnership? Almost certainly. The atmosphere that the scheme had created, the involvement of the players, and the motivation for local kids all contributed to a safer environment.

The community rugby club established at Cougar Park became a model for all kinds of other ambitious clubs, most notably Bradford Rugby League Club. When Super

League arrived, Bradford were the club which embraced its concept most whole-heartedly, under the considerable influence of marketing manager Peter Deakin. He and chairman Chris Caisley were instrumental in turning Northern - the traditional name for the club - into Bulls - the new image - and securing the highest level of community interest of any club in Super League. By its second season, their strategy had boosted attendances to an average of over 15,000. A successful team helped, of course, but the Bullmania that swept Bradford and put horns onto heads and Bullpower into motor cars almost exactly mirrored what happened in Keighley in the mid-1990's. They even set up a community classroom. The big difference, of course, was the size of Bradford's catchment area. While Keighley did well to boost attendances over the 4,000 mark for a league game and up to 7,500 for a cup match, Bradford's potential was seven times greater. In contrast, Keighley's achievement in attracting and maintaining support was far more impressive.

Cougar tactics spread beyond the northern game, though. London bastions of what League supporters like to call the 'rah-rah game,' Harlequins and Richmond, introduced alien concepts such as aggressive public announcements biased towards the home team, and special music for each player when they'd scored. Actually, Keighley's early experiments with celebratory music - what one correspondent to a rugby magazine called *"the tedious accompaniment to every Keighley try"* - featured Queen's *'We will rock you.'* This same piece was heard as half-time ended in the England-Wales international at Twickenham on February 21st 1998. *From Cougar Park to RU HQ!* While it would be foolish to attribute every development of this kind to events in a small Northern town (the adoption of 'personal records' for players in one-day cricket matches was probably borrowed directly from the Southern hemisphere, and Keighley's own ideas were influenced by sports teams in Australia and the United States), they were the first rugby side of either code to seize the future and to shape and influence it. Imitators were sincere in their flattery: In October 1996, for example, top Dutch football club Sparta Rotterdam set up their own classroom based on the Cougar model, following a visit their representatives had made to Keighley.

Peter Deakin's influence didn't end with Bradford. He was head-hunted by Premiership rugby union side Saracens, and set about Cougarising them, too. Millionaire businessman Nigel Wray bankrolled them to such an extent that they were able to buy players of world class like Michael Lynagh and Francois Pienaar, who in 1995 had led their respective countries in the World Cup. But even millionaires - especially millionaires - want a return on their investments, and in order to start pulling in crowds, Saracens moved from their own cosy but poorly-appointed North London ground. After a brief flirtation with Enfield Football Club, they started season 1997-8 at Watford F.C.'s Vicarage Road ground, with a capacity of 22,000. To fund the vast expenditure they've committed themselves to, the club has to pull in the crowds big-time. To do that, Deakin has put certain strategies into practice: players are to make personal appearances at schools, festivals, hospitals and shopping centres - anywhere they can influence potential young supporters or business sponsors: Watford was submerged by Saracens marketing; schoolchildren were offered free tickets and schools that don't play rugby union are being encouraged to take the game up. On the ground during games are lots of features that will be instantly recognisable to Cougars fans: cheerleaders, music, competitions, a giant club mascot (if you're interested, it's a jaffa cake), and a remote-controlled car that brings on the kicking tee. Saracens are taking a terrific gamble, for they're transporting their team to an area that has no natural empathy with rugby, and no team history, unlike Bradford, which had a century of Northern, though the grand old club did go out of existence for one traumatic season. Even so, Deakin's marketing at Saracens was crucial in attracting a crowd of over 14,000 for a league game against Leicester in December 1997.

Attitudes to Keighley in the rest of rugby league were mixed. Some felt their approach at games - loud music and provocative public address - to be brash and disrespectful. Most admired their community programme. As their playing strength improved and the top division seemed an attainable goal, there may well have been a touch of jealousy as some club chairmen realised what the 'upstarts' were achieving.

1993-94: The Awakening

Keighley Cougars began the 1993-4 season as joint 9/4 favourites (with Workington Town) to win the second division. The campaign was heralded locally as *"Cougarmania III - The Awakening,"* and a 27-21 win over Bradford Northern in a pre-season friendly that started half-an-hour late because of the huge crowd trying to get in seemed to justify the optimism. But a win at Barrow was followed by a home defeat (14-17) at the hands of London Crusaders - Keighley's first home reverse since December 1992. The crowd was an impressive 3,200. Six league wins followed, including a 30-20 success at Doncaster, where the attendance of 2,359 was testimony to the growing away support which was to sustain the team all over the league for the next few seasons. Peter Roe was not satisfied with the playing performances, though, and Brendan Hill, the big prop from Halifax, was signed for £20,000 after six weeks on loan. Meanwhile, Cougar TV was launched in the shape of an hour-long programme on a cable network.

Summer signing Greg Austin was proving a huge success, and with 14 tries after 8 games was already threatening Joe Sherburn's 60-year old tryscoring record. Another pointscoring machine, John Wasyliw, hit an individual record with 36 points in the 72-12 Regal Trophy win at home to Nottingham City (he'd set the existing record of 34 against the same hapless opponents a year earlier!) at the end of October, on a day when Cougars celebrated Christmas early with seasonal decorations, all specially for a video that would be released two months later.

As so often, euphoria was followed by despair and then pride. At the beginning of November, Cougars lost at Carlisle in their worst performance of the season, but the Saturday after covered themselves with glory at 1st Division Halifax in the next round of the Regal, putting up a terrific fight in front of a 7,000+ crowd, despite lacking key players through injury.

December and January of that season were horrendous, both on and off the pitch, with two consecutive league defeats, three games postponed - including a lucrative Christmas encounter against Huddersfield, when fans only learned the match was off when they arrived at the ground - and a blood-letting boardroom row. A big crowd on December 7th failed to lift the team as they went down 4-16 at home to Workington, and away fans were hammered by Keighley supporter Trevor Smith for *"bad language and abuse."* Part of the Cougars' strategy in attracting women and children to matches as part of their 'family' atmosphere was to discourage some of the normal patterns of behaviour at rugby games, but this didn't always work with visiting fans, and sometimes goaded them into breaking the Keighley code. To their credit, the Cougars' management have continued to appeal regularly for appropriate vocal support, in much the same way as Brian Clough did at Nottingham Forest. The atmosphere on the terraces at rugby league matches has always been much more friendly than at soccer matches, and Cougar Park is normally a hugely pleasant place to spend a few hours. But success did bring its problems, and there were to be a few acrimonious incidents as possible promotion to Super League became an issue.

Rivalry on the terraces paled into insignificance compared to what was going on in the boardroom. For some time, the ambitions and expansionist activities of Mike Smith and Mick O'Neill had made other directors nervous, as the amounts of money being spent, and the commitments required, began to spiral; the pace of change appalled chairman Ian Mahady and director Trevor Hobson. At the meeting of November 19th 1993, Mahady brought the issue to a head and demanded the resignations of both Smith and O'Neill. He had miscalculated the attitudes of fellow-directors, though, and after a *"rancorous"* argumentative debate, the targetted pair won a narrow 'lack of confidence' vote. Mahady himself was forced to resign, Hobson followed suit, and O'Neill was installed as chairman. Fan Andrew Johnson probably articulated the views of most supporters when he wrote in the following week's *KN* in support of the two Mikes, and an editorial in the same issue pulled no punches: *"Cougars will be stark, raving bonkers to ditch Mike Smith and Mick O'Neill. The club would go back into the dark ages of defeats, debts and perpetual discord."*

The situation was not resolved, however. Ex-chairman Mahady continued to air his views, and called a special shareholders' meeting, which was eventually scheduled for January 18th. In the meantime, he emphasised what the issues were: *"They (Smith and O'Neill) have great ideas, and nobody can question their enthusiasm for the club, but they are not suitable people to be on the board of directors."* Most of the arguments, of course, were about money, and the alleged spending of what the club didn't immediately possess. *"The club has to be run on a sound basis... though the town and the spectators want success; we all do."* Mike Smith, though, was not going to lie down. He prepared an hour-long video showing what had already been achieved, presented it at the start of the

Martin Wood *was born at Streethouse on 24th June 1970 and played amateur rugby with Featherstone Miners Welfare and Streethouse before turning professional with Halifax, making his debut in the 1988/89 season. Martin's best season with Halifax was the 1990/91 season when he scored 31 tries, including one in the 2nd Division Premiership Final at Old Trafford, when Halifax were defeated by Salford. Halifax had gained promotion to the 1st Division, but Martin was not given the opportunity to show his skills at the top flight and moved to Scarborough Pirates for a short spell before joining Keighley in January 1992. Martin was always confident that he could compete at the top level and hoped to prove it with Keighley. He played his part in taking Keighley to the 3rd Division Championship in the 1992/93 season and the 2nd Division Championship in the 1994/95 season. Primarily operating in the loose forward position, but also effective as a stand-off, Martin made 151 appearances for Keighley, scoring 85 tries, 25 goals and 3 drop goals, making a total of 393 points for the club. As well as winning two Championship medals with Keighley, he also appeared in two Divisional Premiership finals at Old Trafford, being on the winning side once. Martin finally got his chance to show he was capable of competing at the highest level when he moved on to Sheffield Eagles before the start of the 1997 season.*

special meeting, and guaranteed the backing of shareholders when it came time to vote. Cougarmania was back on track. Ironically, this dispute had erupted while the magnificent new £200,000 clubhouse was taking shape. And curiously, the *KN* still lapsed into referring to the ground as 'Lawkholme Lane'!

3,190 watched Cougars beat Rochdale 40-12 on the following Saturday, though attendances at the next two home games were lower, at around 2,200 each; this could have had as much to do with the quality of the opposition (Oulton, in the Challenge Cup, and Barrow) and the weather as the behind-the-scenes traumas. After a second-round Challenge Cup win at Batley, 5,278 turned up in midweek to see the re-arranged match against Huddersfield, which Keighley convincingly won 35-10. The draw for the third round of the Cup pulled out a home draw against mighty Castleford, and for the next ten days, the town really did go Cougar crazy, with mega-hype and media coverage. All 4,000 tickets allocated to home fans were sold out in three hours. Unfortunately, the team couldn't deliver; The game was over as a contest within 20 minutes, and Cas won 52-14.

Cougars had hauled themselves back into the promotion race, which was hotting up, but after regaining a foothold, they contrived to slip up immediately, with defeats at Dewsbury, London and Whitehaven, and a draw at home to Doncaster. At the end of March came a real low-point: the home game against Batley (a 6-22 loss) featured the worst brawl seen at the ground for years, as all 26 players on the field slugged it out for five minutes.

Coach Peter Roe, disappointed with the failure to achieve a second successive promotion, parted company with the club. Smith called his performance over the previous three seasons *"intelligent, emotive and incisive,"* but the club was determined to achieve the top flight in rugby league, and Roe had failed to deliver the desired second success. He left after a period with the club which had seen a massive transformation on the playing side, and was generous in his praise of Smith and O'Neill: *"They have put their heart and soul into Keighley and deserve every success."*

The team made the premiership play-offs, but suffered a humiliating 12-66 defeat at London. Over a thousand Keighley supporters made the journey to the capital, and Mick O'Neill was forced to apologise for *"a terrible, insipid performance; it was absolutely disgraceful."* The only consolation from the game was that Nick Pinkney broke the club try-scoring record with his 31st of the season. Austin, who had earlier looked likeliest to break it, had left the club in mid-season after an acrimonious dispute about contracts and wages.

The first important task of the close season was to find a successor coach to Peter Roe. Various names were rumoured to be on the brink of signing: Roger Millward, Tony Gordon, and David Topliss all appeared to be in the frame, but when the actual signing came, it was a publicity coup par excellence because of the sheer surprise of it. Phil Larder was no ordinary mortal. The 'iron man' of rugby league, the perfectionist, the guy who had coached at the highest level. *"The most exciting signing the club has made in a hundred years,"* enthused Mick O'Neill. He and Mike Smith, having decided that Larder would be of immense benefit to the Cougars, drove to Widnes and telephoned their target from a phone box outside Naughton Park, the Widnes ground. They persuaded Larder to talk to them, and in discussions with Phil and his wife Anne, completely Cougarised them. The deal was done. Keighley's capture sent shock waves through the game, especially at Widnes, where his contract apparently had some time to run. It also seemed likely to send shockwaves through the Cougars' playing staff. *"They* (the players) *will work harder than they have ever worked in their lives,"* announced Larder. *"If I don't get the commitment I expect, they will be moving on."* He immediately forecast promotion at the end of the coming season, and made it clear he'd joined Keighley because they were seemingly a club of limitless ambition. It appeared that one player who might not figure in the new coach's plans was Ian Gately, who had just been voted 'Player of the year' in the supporters' club awards. Both he and Andy Eyres were out of contract. In the event, the big prop did enough in early appearances the following season to change Larder's mind. Another prop wanted to move of his own accord: Steve Hall was bitterly disappointed that the club hadn't achieved instant promotion to the top flight, and requested a transfer. The new coach persuaded him that his best interest was to stay and help the club achieve it the next time round.

Larder says he came to Keighley because it was an up and coming, exciting club, and he was impressed with the whole aura of Cougermania. He was given a remit to sort out everything on the playing side and he felt the management was sound, selling the game and the team within the community - though he was soon to realise that things weren't quite so rosy as he first imagined.

Nick Pinkney was born in Hull on 6th December 1970 and joined Hull Dockers at 13 years of age; with them he represented Yorkshire at all levels and Great Britain Under 18's. Nick started his professional career with Hull K.R. Colts before moving on to Ryedale-York in July 1990, where he represented Great Britain Under 21s against Papua New Guinea. When he joined Keighley on 13th May 1993, Nick was a noted try scorer, having scored 54 in 95 appearances for Ryedale-York, but I don't think anyone appreciated just what a prolific try scorer he was going to turn out to be with Keighley. Whilst with the Cougars, Nick earned international honours, winning four caps, including three appearances in the 1995 World Cup competition. As a centre threequarter with Keighley, his blistering pace brought him a total of 101 tries in just 103 appearances, breaking several club records in the process. Twice in the 1994/95 season, Nick scored five tries in a match to equal the record set by Ike Jagger in 1906 and Sam Stacey in 1907, although this standard was subsequently beaten by Jason Critchley in 1996. One record, however was smashed out of sight. His 45 tries in the 1994/95 season easily eclipsed his previous best of 31, set the previous season which, in turn, had beaten Joe Sherburn's 30 scored in the 1934/35 season. Along with Martin Wood, Nick Pinkney's association with Keighley was ended with his transfer to Sheffield Eagles before the start of the 1997 season.

Meanwhile, Magnet Trade confirmed their sponsorship for another season, with the firm's director Ray Hammond emphasising that it was important for businesses to put something into their local sports teams. A successful town club, he asserted, put a spring in the step of everyone in the community. Down at the ground, plans for the 'Hard Knock Cafe' and burger bar/nightclub were taking shape. Bill Spencer, the longest-serving club official - he had become club secretary in 1954 - stepped down from the Board, and was immediately made the club's first honorary president.

The summer before what was to be Keighley's pinnacle season was hugely eventful, with the club making the front pages for quite the wrong reasons. May saw a row between the club and one of its ex-directors, Carol Jessop. Carol had been running the club shop, but after a blazing row with other directors over allocation of tickets for the previous season's cup game with Castleford, resigned from the board. The club alleged she had removed Cougar merchandise from the club shop and was selling it at cut-price rates in her own retail outlet, *Instyle*, competing directly and unfairly against the club itself. A month later, there was another of the regular cash crisis stories. The club was desperate for money to complete the 'Hard Knock Cafe', the pitch needed a total repair of drains and surface, and the development of a new stand to replace the old 'scrattin' shed' needed financing. The directors asked Bradford Metropolitan Council for a grant of £150,000, but this was turned down on the grounds that the club was 'technically insolvent.' O'Neill pointed out that the council supported Bradford Northern to a greater financial extent, but the Council retorted that they had always been generous in their support for the Cougars. This argument was to run and run through the summer and the following season. Immediately, a scheme was devised to finance the pitch drainage plan, which was expected to cost £22,000: local businesses would be asked to cough up £1,000 to sponsor a new 'strip.' In the event, few of these were taken up, but it was typical of much of the directors' strategy. Each financial problem was tackled with an imaginative fund-raising effort. This could be interpreted either as enterprise or poor forward planning, but it often worked. Sometimes it looked like living from hand to mouth.

Shortage of cash, however, did not hinder more player signings. In June, Andre Stoop came from London Crusaders - though his first visit to Keighley was not an auspicious one. Stoop found it so cold he went straight back to London, and one of the directors had to follow the disgruntled player to persuade him to return. Promising youngsters Gareth Cochrane from Hull and Darren Fleary from Dewsbury were signed in July, followed by possibly Larder's shrewdest signing, Chris Robinson from Halifax. Oldham's Shane Tupaea came along in August.

These new signings were financed largely by injections of cash by millionaire businessman Richard Padgett and John Smith, another well-heeled business colleague. Otherwise the club was in a parlous financial state. Former player Allan Clarkson joined the board at the end of July, and a week later director Ronnie Moore resigned. The new directors had been coaxed on board after Bradford Council had turned down yet another plea for cash. New coach Larder had decided the squad needed strengthening and, as usual, the cupboard was bare. At least the pitch resurfacing was taking shape, and the club had a cast of players that looked quite capable of winning promotion from the second division.

In early 1994, David Bailey, who had been a director twice during the eighties, had been installed as chief executive, and that summer was left in charge as the entire board disappeared on various holidays. It was the first week of Phil Larder's time at the club, and a whole host of financial problems quickly became apparent to Bailey. One morning, the telephone in his office failed to work, having been cut off after several warnings. David hurried into town to pay the outstanding £900 out of his own pocket in order to get the phone line re-instated before the new coach suspected there might be anything wrong. Larder had been told that £100,000 was available to spend on new players - yet the telephone bill had not been paid.

Mike Smith was interviewed in depth in *Open Rugby* magazine of April 1994, and set out his views on the promotion of Rugby League, which he said was still perceived by many people as *"a bunch of fat blokes running around on a muddy field."* The game, he said, had to be properly marketed, and he cited Cougars as the only British club that was market-led and had really tried to promote the game properly in its catchment area. *"The Cougars want to put the fun back into the game."* He advocated summer rugby - but only after careful planning to initiate it in, say, three years time - and argued that, although tradition was important, the future lay in attracting young spectators.

"The Keighley Cougars have become the 'buzz words' in British Rugby League when it comes to self-promotion and taking the game to the people. Their story has been a remarkable tribute to those involved." (Open Rugby magazine, April 1994)

1994-95: The Triumph

Phil Larder

Cougarmania IV began with the traditional pre-season friendly for the Joe Phillips Trophy against local rivals Bradford Northern. After two successive wins, Keighley were looking for a hat-trick. In the event, they were denied by a last-minute converted try, which gave Northern a last-minute draw on their final visit to Cougar Park under their old name. When are they likely to appear again now? Larder professed himself *"delighted"* with the performance; his charges would, he was sure, be meeting Bradford twice in the first division the following season. The first league game at home went smoothly, Cougars disposing of Whitehaven 38-8, with half-backs Robinson and Eyres outstanding. The kick-off was delayed for 15 minutes to get the crowd (3,170) in, though this was partly the club's fault. The directors had made a decision to suspend the council's 'Passport to Leisure' scheme, which allowed cheap admission for children, concessionaires and

> *Team for the first home game of 1994-95 was Stoop; Kenyon, Pinkney, Creaser, Walker; Eyres, Robinson; Gately, Ramshaw, Hall, Fleary, Tupaea, Stephenson. Subs: Appleby, Wood.*

pensioners to events within Bradford Met that the council sponsored. Cougars hadn't, however, announced the end of the concession, and people only found out when they arrived, so causing some heated discussion at the turnstiles and a consequent delay. The council was furious, though Mike Smith claimed the Cougars were *"not a charity."* Later, a compromise was reached, but it was a poor public relations start to the season. Phil Larder, never one to pull his punches, was highly critical of the referee for the Whitehaven game who, he alleged, had failed to protect his team from the visitors' over-aggressive and intimidatory tactics. In his *Larder at Large* column in the local paper, he claimed referees should *"understand the game, not just the rules."* Larder stayed in the news by turning down the Great Britain coaching job on the grounds that he wanted an all-British back-up staff. A 30-16 success at Rochdale followed, with the vast majority of the 2,111 crowd Cougar fans. This pattern of terrific away support was to be repeated through the season, intensifying as events reached boiling point in April. The travelling fans provided the home clubs with a cash bonanza, something the Rugby League consistently failed to appreciate or acknowledge later. Larder was less happy with the next home game, a draw against Ryedale-York in front of 3,350 spectators. Larder apologised in his column and then, provocative as ever, criticised the Rugby League for wanting London (now called the Broncos, after a take-over by Brisbane owner Barry Maranta) in the top flight. While it was desirable to have a rugby league side in the capital, the special rules that allowed them to field a full side of Australians were unfair. As Keighley were due to visit the Broncos the following week, this might be thought to have been tempting fate, but Cougars, exuding confidence, signed Simon Irving from Leeds, gave him his debut at London, and were delighted by his performance, which helped Keighley win 30-10. Irving, an ex- rugby union player, cost £35,000, and was to prove another shrewd signing, working wonders at Cougar Park as player, captain and assistant coach, until events in the summer of 1997 saw him return to Leeds.

"As a second division club, the way that you promote the game is to be applauded. The D.J. does an amazing job of encouraging the existing enthusiasm both before and during the game. I had heard a great deal about the enthusiasm for the game at Keighley, but was pleasantly surprised at the degree. The men and women of the backroom staff must be really dedicated."
(Castleford supporter, March 1994)

A couple of days after the London game, the Rugby League came out with its first bombshell of the season. The 'Framing the Future' document that arose from the findings of a committee deputed to investigate a restructuring of the game recommended that only one side should be promoted from Division 2 at the end of the season. This, of course, was to put much more pressure on all the challenging sides. Further, the document suggested that teams in the future 'premiership,' as it was envisaged the top division would be called, should have grounds with a 10,000 minimum capacity, with 2,500 seated and 6,000 undercover. This, if implemented, would have excluded Keighley, who could not match those specifications. Cougars played the rest of the season with at least one of these threats hanging over their heads.

Both the one-club promotion rule and ground capacity minimum figure were presumably designed to raise standards of the clubs in the top flight. Yet the rationale was badly thought-out. Any artificial attempt to exclude particular clubs from the top division when they had got there on merit was unfair and irrational. The Premier Football League didn't exclude Wimbledon, even when they didn't have a ground, and The Rugby Football Union were hardly likely to kick Bath out of their Premiership because their ground capacity was only about 8,000. In the cloud cuckoo land of rugby league, where grand ideas come cheap, any U-turns or flights of fantasy are possible.

All this was put in the background as Cougars beat Dewsbury at home (crowd approaching 4,000) and Bramley - with an unimpressive performance - away, where four-fifths of the spectators were from Keighley. The side went to the top of the division for the first time, and then travelled to Barrow, who were coached by Peter Roe. Larder slammed the home team's tactics and attitude, and claimed his predecessor *"lost the respect of the Keighley players"* that day. The 24-10 win was followed by a disappointing 22-26 home reverse to Batley, with the *"worst defensive performance of the season."* (Larder). The attendance of 4,298, though, was the fourth best in the whole league on that particular Sunday. The day before, the Rugby League had changed its mind on promotion: two sides would go up. Yet the impression remained that, given the 'Framing the Future' ground criteria, these might not necessarily be the two sides that finished at the top of the table. Many people already felt that London Broncos would be promoted wherever they finished at the end of the season.

Meanwhile, supporters were now getting the chance to watch a video of each game on Monday nights at the clubhouse, and it was announced that Cougars were reinforcing the war against drugs: The drugs and alcohol agency Project Six was working with the town's rugby league team to train local teenagers to be 'peer educators.' The Cougar classroom was also thriving. Arrangements were in full swing to take another army of children to Wembley for the forthcoming Test match against Australia. The £15 a head charge (the previous season it had been £5, because local businesses had sponsored the trip) was to include free admission to games at Cougar Park for the rest of the season. In the event, 1,118 younsters went in a huge convoy of coaches, a feat that any other club might have emulated, with imagination.

The home reverse against Batley was to be the last of 1994, for Cougars began to turn in some spectacular performances. A 66-10 success at home to Hunslet included five Nick Pinkney tries, and big wins against Carlisle and Whitehaven followed. The club tried to extend its catchment area by encouraging lads from Asian families in the Lawkholme area to come to Cougar Park. Mary Calvert arranged for groups to be shown round the ground by Grant Doorey as part of a general promotion of the club.

In late November, Keighley's MP Gary Waller featured in the *KN* as *'Fan of the week,'* a regular series which spotlighted supporters and their views each week. Waller promised to run the London Marathon the following year in a Cougar shirt. He enthusiastically supported the club. *"Keighley had not had much to celebrate for a long time. The success of the Cougars gave everyone a tremendous uplift."*

The only black spots at this time of euphoria both on the playing side and in the community programme were the pitch itself, still dreadful despite the £25,000 drainage scheme, which appeared to have been a complete failure, and a strange story that former coach Peter Roe was taking the club to an industrial tribunal for *"constructive dismissal."* The state of the pitch did not prevent Cougars chalking up wins in the first two rounds of the Regal Trophy, lining up an appetising third round tie at home to first division side Sheffield Eagles. Keighley warmed themselves up for this task by demolishing Ryedale-York 52-12 with a super display of *"pace, handling and control."* The team's exploits were attracting the attention of the national press, and in a typical piece, *The Guardian*'s Paul Fitzpatrick, homed in on Keighley. Under the headline, *'Daring to dream with the Cougars'*, Fitzpatrick admired the heady cocktail of community involvement, charismatic coach and exciting marketing, and called Keighley *"a remarkable club."* The Eagles didn't have a chance with the Cougars on such a roll, and in what Phil Larder called *"an awesome first half,"* laid the foundations for an impressive 26-10 win before 3,914 spectators. With tries from Dixon, Cochrane and Robinson, and four goals from Irving, they were ahead 20-0 by the interval. *"I didn't think I would see anything as brilliant as that at Keighley,"* enthused director Mike Smith. In a sense, the balance of power in rugby league changed that day. Keighley were now seen to be capable of taking on the best, a realisation that would be confirmed in the next round. Sheffield boss Gary Hetherington could not have failed to be impressed with what he saw at Cougar Park that afternoon - the standard of rugby, the atmosphere, the passionate involvement. On Boxing Day, a near 5,000 crowd watched a 24-12 win over Hull K.R., the twelfth league success in fourteen games. The team was well on course for winning Division Two, and the local paper's end-of-year report gave Cougars 'A' for entertainment - but rather less for economics. Perhaps it was time for another share issue?

New Year's Eve had Cougars at Huddersfield, beating fellow promotion contenders Huddersfield 15-10 in *"an intense second division performance,"* a game that encouraged optimism for the Regal Trophy fourth-round tie, where Keighley had drawn another first division side, Warrington, at home. A bumper crowd of 5,600 watched spellbound as Cougars led going into the last seconds of the game, only to be beaten by a piece of Jonathan Davies magic. Once again, Cougars showed they were up with the top clubs:

"The Keighley College/ Cougars partnership brought some welcome Christmas spirit to children and staff at Airedale Hospital on Monday. A monster chocolate snowman was handed over for their Christmas party, and club captain Joe Grima, alongside team-mates Ian Gately and Kevin Marr, was on hand to answer questions and bring a special 'Cougar Christmas' to the children." (Adrian Heath, December 1993)

perhaps the hierarchy of the game were beginning to get a little bit nervous. Prop Steve Hall's dream went that day, as well, though: he fractured a leg in two places during the game. Four days later, it was perhaps not surprising that the side lost 14-25 at home to London Broncos, a reaction from the intensity of the previous two games.

Behind the scenes, the momentum showed no sign of abating, as a new life members' scheme was launched against the background of a report that the club was £100,000 in debt. On the first day of the scheme, over £30,000 was pledged, with director Mike Smith urging that Keighley were *"standing on the threshold of the biggest opportunity this club has ever known."* Ten days later, a £1 million ground development plan was unveiled, to include a new grandstand on the old scrattin' shed side of the ground - some contrast with the £450 it cost to put up the shed in 1937. This scheme never got off the ground, but it was typical of Smith and O'Neill's constant search for improvement and progress in their usual *unveil the plan, then find the money* style. Meanwhile, the pitch itself was in a shocking state. Only tons of sand spread over the surface - which gave it the bizarre appearance of a seaside beach - kept the show on the road at home until the end of the season.

February began with another comfortable league win, this time against Leigh, and Nick Pinkney was selected for the England squad to play France at Gateshead. He played - and, naturally, scored. In the next league game, a 24-8 success at home to Bramley, Nick equalled his club try-scoring record of the previous season, then passed it as Keighley beat Dewsbury 24-12 in the second round of the Challenge Cup.

The atmosphere at home games continued to be marvellous, fired by O'Neill on the microphone. The home players came out at the start of each half with a public address roar *"It's Coo..oou..garr...time."* Players had personal records which were played enthusiastically after each score. Everyone in the ground was cougarised. It was impossible not to be.

By now, Keighley were five points clear at the top of Division Two, and promotion was looking an excellent bet. A curious feature of the season's games, though, was the fact that the atmosphere at away games was sometimes better than at home matches, with the committed travellers getting behind the team throughout the eighty minutes. Over at RL headquarters, the sands continued to shift. A report prepared by Gary Hetherington, the man who had nurtured Sheffield Eagles to be a force in the game, and who was respected as coach and thinker on the game, had prepared a report advocating a switch to summer rugby. Few people at Keighley would have argued against that principle in the weeks to come.

Another international call-up from Cougar Park was the drafting of Gareth Cochrane into the under-21 squad. Further interest was provided by rumours of an imminent signing of a top player. That story didn't come to fruition until the beginning of April, and when the news finally broke, it was indeed sensational...

The impression from the following five weeks was that another inspirational player was certainly needed. Despite Phil Larder's injunction to his team before the second round cup game on the last Sunday in February to be *"totally focused,"* the home game against Huddersfield (attendance 5,700) was a complete anti-climax, Cougars losing 0-30, with the visitors looking superior in every position on the day. Keighley played Huddersfield four times that season, and three of the games were classics: this cup game was just a nightmare. March 1995 was a hugely disappointing month, with the promotion drive faltering as three league matches were lost. There were two heavily mitigating factors, though. The club had a horrendous injury list, and the weather was not suiting Keighley's fluent style; other sides who would have been totally outclassed in early season conditions were able to seriously trouble Cougars. At Batley, a frozen pitch made the game a lottery, one which promotion rivals Batley won 8-6. Wins at home to Highfield and away to Hunslet followed, but then came two games where Keighley failed to score a try. A big band of supporters went to Dewsbury in midweek to provide the bulk of a 3,395 crowd, but the team failed to deliver, losing 2-20 in a performance which coach Larder labelled as *"the worst I've ever been associated with."* The Dewsbury public address cruelly played *'The party's over...'* as the game ended, and when Keighley lost 2-12 at Carlisle four days later, it seemed that it might indeed be. In both matches, though, conditions were terrible. Even so, the 'Cougar Champions' flags were put on hold.

As so often during the Cougar years, however, management and players had a happy knack of coming up with a little bit of magic to lighten the gloom whenever things got too heavy. The team did it with two super performances - at Leigh, winning 34-13, and at home to Swinton - and all the doubts about promotion were lifted at a stroke. And in early April came the biggest signing in the club's history, the confirmation of weeks of rumour. The *Keighley News* proclaimed *"The Eagle has landed,"* in a classic headline. Daryl

"I thoroughly enjoyed my week at Cougar Park on work experience, and found it very interesting. The staff, especially Mary Calvert, who I shadowed, were very friendly and made me feel extremely welcome and part of their team. I was surprised by how much goes on as before I only saw the club from the terraces on a cold Sunday afternoon. Thanks." (Hannah Fleming, South Craven School, March 1994)

Powell, Great Britain international and one of the biggest names in the game, had signed. The cost, of course, was prohibitive, at £130,000, nearly four times as much as Keighley's previous record signing, Pinkney. *"I'm still shaking,"* said Mick O'Neill days afterwards. Powell was also found a job with Mike Smith's cable TV company. Much of the money probably came from the recently-promoted life membership scheme, and commercial manager Norma Rankin contacted all major sponsors and shareholders and asked them for help in financing the deal. The necessary was soon raised. Daryl Powell was to be the final piece in the jigsaw that would see Keighley survive in the First Division, to which they were surely now headed. The aims were getting more ambitious all the time: Cougars were now being put on track to be one of rugby league's top five teams.

Four days later, the bombshell exploded.

Super League shut-out

On Saturday 8th April, the chairmen of all 32 professional rugby league clubs, along with those of three recently axed from the league, met at Wigan to make a decision about a plan that many of them knew little or nothing about before they arrived. Faxed instructions had been sent just 36 hours earlier. Some chairmen didn't get the meeting details until early on Saturday morning. What the second division bosses didn't know was that a meeting of 'top' clubs had already taken place the day before, and that they were to be presented with what in effect was a *fait accompli.*

On April 4th, at the same time that the Powell deal was finally going through, Maurice Lindsay, the chief executive of the Rugby League, was talking to representatives of Rupert Murdoch's News Corporation BSkyB television company about an offer they'd made to fund the game in Britain for five years. A European Super League (in which News Corp originally wanted just ten teams) and summer rugby were the basic ingredients, and the initial offer was £50 million, negotiated to £75 million. Once the offer was on the table, events moved with breathtaking speed, and by the time of the Wigan meeting four days later, the real decisions had already been taken. Quite why BSkyB insisted on the deal being rushed through is unclear, but a possible explanation is that Murdoch, for whom the takeover of British rugby league was merely a tactical step in his TV war in Australia with rival station Channel 9, wanted a deal settled promptly to underpin his Australian coup. Lindsay and RL chairman Rodney Walker (who at the time was also Sports Council chairman) were worried that a delay in accepting the deal might mean that they'd lose the News Corporation offer, which was subsequently (by 30th April) upped to £87 million. They concocted a plan for a 'Super League', which was refined at a meeting of the Rugby League Council at Headingley the day after Lindsay received the original offer, and determined that the widely-touted move to summer rugby should take place at the same time. The second of these ideas was becoming acceptable to many clubs already, but the former plan, when it was released to a secret meeting of First Division clubs (along with Hull Kingston Rovers) on the evening of Friday 7th April at Huddersfield, was highly contentious. When it was presented to the media in the following week, it caused an outrage in most rugby league centres. The Lindsay-Walker Super League was based on News Corporation's demand for a slimmed-down elite club structure and was to include two French clubs and one in South Wales (which at the time didn't exist), London Broncos (below Keighley in Division Two), five existing first division clubs and - astonishingly - five new clubs in the north formed by mergers of existing ones. The fusion of Castleford, Featherstone and Wakefield was a proposal that came straight out of cloud cuckoo land, and expecting Warrington and Widnes to end a century-old rivalry and hold hands was quite ridiculous.

At the Saturday meeting of all the clubs, Mick O'Neill listened to the proposed outline with mounting horror, and phoned Phil Larder as soon as he realised that Keighley were not to be included in any Super League plan. Worse, there was to be no promotion to this elite division for at least two seasons. The Cougars were to be shut out again. Despite their being constantly quoted as being a credit to the sport, despite the fact that their marketing strategy was being imitated by lots of other clubs, despite their promotion of rugby league to a wider audience, despite the fact that they were making national headlines for their initiatives..... the door to promotion was effectively closed. This was not, as Lindsay had made clear at the start of the Wigan meeting, a subject for negotiation. He stated clearly that if a decision wasn't reached immediately, the Murdoch offer would be withdrawn. The chairmen had to vote yes or else - this was not a consultation exercise. The whole deal had already been approved by First Division chairmen, anyway. This original plan envisaged that the whole of the News Corporation money would go to Super

"The relationship between players and fans here is special. It amazes me the time it takes players to leave the field after the match....Division One is just around the corner."
(Graham Colley, Radio Leeds, October 1994)

League clubs only. Every club except Chorley voted in favour of acceptance, though this does not mean they agreed with what was going on: O'Neill felt that the only way he could fight the plan was by staying inside it.

The news, announced by Mick O'Neill on the pitch at Cougar Park before the Swinton game on April 9th, caused uproar in Keighley. The phrase *"sold out"* was most frequently used. MP Gary Waller called the deal *"an appalling and unforgivable betrayal."* The *KN* was scathing: *"Murdoch dangled a £75m. carrot...Lindsay and his advisors scoffed it with indecent haste."* A cartoon showed Murdoch riding on Lindsay's back past a Cougar in a second division cage. A protest meeting was called and took place on the evening of Monday 10th April at the ground, when 2,000 fans promised to start a 'people-power campaign.' Typically, the team had produced its best performance for months the day before in beating Swinton 42-6 in front of a big 4,221 crowd.

The *KN*, predictably, was flooded with Cougar letters, a mixture of anger, frustration, and bewilderment - along with praise for what the club had achieved. One fan, Tim Wood of Ilkley, was prepared to take up Maurice Lindsay's dictum that clubs with bigger stadiums would get Super League preference by suggesting a move to Turf Moor, Burnley F.C.'s ground. Keighley moving to Lancashire? Desperation indeed, though the idea was mooted again during Carl Metcalfe's chairmanship in 1996. *"Keighley Cougars, praised as the innovators of modern rugby league, should have been one of the first names in the Super League,"* thundered David Melbourne, *"that they have been excluded is nothing less than criminal."*

Supporters were still optimistic that the decision to exclude Keighley from Super League could be reversed, however. Maurice Lindsay indicated on 12th April that if Keighley could raise £1.5 million within 48 hours (an indication that they would be well underpinned financially), he would reconsider their 'application' for Super League. Mick O'Neill, never one to duck a challenge, set about negotiations with his bank, putting up his house as part of the collateral for such a loan, and just before the expiry of the ridiculous time limit, obtained a letter from the bank stating that the required amount would be available. He drove to Lindsay's office in Leeds, only to find the chief executive leaving for Manchester. Undeterred, O'Neill followed Lindsay along the M62, walked into a meeting that was taking place with Chris Caisley, Bradford Bulls chairman, and showed the bank letter to an astonished Lindsay. It did not, however, make any difference to league policy. The door to the Super League was going to be firmly shut.

Mary Calvert was detailed to put together a presentation putting forward Keighley's case for Super League inclusion. Despite some compelling arguments, this had no effect. Mary recalls very strongly the feeling of helplessness as successive hurdles were cleared, only for others to be erected in their place. Statements around this time alleged to have been made by Lindsay and Bradford chairman Chris Caisley were patronising and insulting to a club that had pioneered community involvement. Maurice Lindsay: *"Everyone has a soft spot for such an enterprising little club* (as Keighley)*, but we are planning a Super League, not a sympathy league."* Caisley: *"Now and again there is a need to step out of Cougarland, put your feet on the ground, and get into the real world."* This latter was from the chairman of a club which, as the Bulls, modelled its promotional ideas on much of what Keighley had done in the early 1990's.

"Not since Queen Victoria mispronounced Keighley as Keely have the eyes of the world been on the town - and it has conducted itself brilliantly" wrote the KN. Cougarmania certainly hit the House of Commons as M.P. Gary Waller persuaded the all-party RL Group to denounce the Super League plan in Parliament. During a Commons debate on the issue, Waller urged that the plan should be referred to the Monopolies and Mergers Commission. He was supported by M.P.s Alice Mahon (Halifax) and Gerry Sutcliffe (Bradford South) from other league towns. Sports minister Ian Sproat was sympathetic. The name of Bradford Bulls chairman Chris Caisley made frequent incursions into the debate, particularly as he had criticised the all-party group as *"wolves in sheep's clothing."* Waller outlined the positive results that had flowed from the Keighley club's activities, both on the field and in the town. The group was concerned that the sport was selling itself entirely to News Corporation, and representatives went to see Maurice Lindsay and Rodney Walker, putting the view that they felt decisions had been made without fans being properly consulted.

In Keighley, legal moves against the League were being put into effect, and the club established a 'fighting fund' to meet an expected £50,000 which would be needed to fund an action fronted by top London barrister Jonathan Crystal. Worth Brewery promised to donate 5p for every pint of Alesman bitter sold, and donations from individuals flooded into Barclays Bank in the town. The supporters' club, loyal and hardworking as ever, contributed a significant amount of money to the cause. Once again, supporters were putting their money behind the club.

Phil Larder feels that, although *"Murdoch blew Keighley out of the water,"* Keighley may not have handled the situation the best way by reacting so strongly. There was a great admiration within the game for everything that the club had done and for the way in which it had built up its support base, but the resort to legal action alienated other clubs - and the Rugby Football League. In retrospect, patience might have been a better option. He is in no doubt, however, that Keighley would have survived in Super League; in fact he's certain they would have been well-placed to secure a place in the top half of the table in that first SL season. *"But,"* said Mick O'Neill, *"what else did they expect us to do?"* For the second time in three seasons, Keighley had legitimately won promotion to a higher division, only to find the rules changed towards the end of the season. The club that was the supreme example of promotion of the game wasn't to be allowed the rewards.

The Cougars acknowledge their fans at Spotland after the record 104-4 victory over Highfield (photo: Graham Smith)

Maurice Lindsay, too, said that Keighley's aggressive attitude won them few friends at a time when many clubs were fighting for their very existence. The original merger plan would have guaranteed all the 1994-95 First Division teams a place in Super League, but, in the case of many of them, as part of a joint club with a new name. By April 30th, some of those clubs were to be shut out as well. It seemed amazing that some actual rugby was going on at the same time, but indeed it was, as the team aimed to confirm its top of the table position. 3,000 supporters travelled to the game at Hull Kingston Rovers on Good Friday, when Cougars won 14-6, and three days later, over 5,200 were at Cougar Park to see a thrilling 22-22 draw with Huddersfield.

The players parade the 1994-95 Second Division Trophy as their open-top bus tour reaches Cavendish Street (photo: Graham Smith)

Just one match remained - away to Highfield, who arranged to switch the match to Spotland, home of Rochdale Football Club, so that more fans could be accommodated as Keighley sought to confirm themselves as Second Division champions. The day was unforgettable: virtually all 4,500 of the crowd came from East of the Pennines, and Cougars destroyed Highfield with a record score in a match between two professional rugby league teams. The atmosphere at the game was one that any Super League team would have been envious of. Nick Pinkney scored five tries, and Andy Eyres and Jason Ramshaw three each, with 12 conversions from Simon Irving in a mammoth 104-4 score. Less than three years on, Highfield, who became Prescot Panthers, are out of the league altogether. The Spotland game sent an urgent message to Maurice Lindsay: *"Cougarmania is alive and will not be beaten!"* The championship celebrations continued at Cougar Park until the early hours of the morning.

The last chance

Rumours of changes of mind by the Rugby League abounded as lawyer Crystal vowed *"to go for the throat."* Were Keighley about to be offered a Super League place after all? Would SL be upped to 20 clubs? The fighting fund had raised £6,000 by the end of April, and court action looked likely.

The original Super League plans had come in for immense criticism, particularly from those clubs who were earmarked for merger. Supporters of clubs like Featherstone and Widnes made it absolutely clear that they wanted nothing to do with a joint operation with a rival neighbour club, and club chairmen, who had approved the News Corporation deal on April 8th, were having rapid second thoughts. So, too, was the Rugby League, which called another special meeting for April 30th. In the intervening 22 days, a compromise of major proportions was worked out. This compromise was outlined to Keighley on April 29th, day of the Challenge Cup Final, at a meeting in a London hotel, with Mike Smith, Mick O'Neill, Rodney Walker and Maurice Lindsay among those present.

"The Cougar fans make all our matches into home games." (Simon Irving, February 1995)

The new plan was outlined to all club chairmen the following day. The idea of enforced mergers was dropped, there would be three divisions - Super League and two others - and a guaranteed promotion place for the winner of the First Division at the end of the first summer season in 1996. Additionally, an extra £12 million had been secured from the Sky deal, money which would be distributed to clubs throughout the league (an amended proposal from the original plan), though Super League clubs would take the bulk. Super League was to consist of 12 clubs, ten of those who had been in the previous First Division, with the addition of London and Paris. The compromise meant that Featherstone, Wakefield, Widnes and Salford, which had all failed to agree on any merger proposals, would lose their top flight status. Faced with the argument that the game, near bankrupt, might collapse entirely without the money offered over five years, three of those clubs joined all but one of the rest in voting in favour of the compromise. Widnes, for whom exclusion was a particularly bitter pill to swallow - they had never been outside the top division - voted against. Keighley abstained, Mick O'Neill staying out of the meeting, unable to approve a deal which he felt the town and supporters would see as a betrayal. Keighley's intransigence annoyed some clubs, who felt that their highly public stance might jeopardise the TV deal, and Lindsay has scant sympathy for their opposition. *"Keighley were given every opportunity to deal with the situation democratically, but refused to vote. I get disappointed when people make the club out to be a martyr. It is just unfortunate that Keighley won promotion at a time when the game was being restructured, but it was the democratic wish of the game at the time."*

Widnes, having voted against the compromise, took their case against expulsion from the top flight to the courts, but a judge ruled that as the decision had been taken by representatives of all member clubs, it was perfectly proper. Once Widnes's action collapsed, Keighley dropped theirs, too.

But in essence, although the KN and some of its readers pronounced themselves satisfied with this deal, the basic fact remained that Keighley had been denied a promotion that they had earned, and that London Broncos, three places behind them at the end of the season, had got one. The directors initially refused to sign their agreement to this deal, and it was early July before Neil Spencer put his signature to the paper which confirmed Keighley's place in the First Division for the following summer, the first outing for the new post-Murdoch system.

Opinion in the town was divided on the issue. Some supporters clearly felt that Cougars might be better off in a smaller Division One, playing quality opposition such as Salford, Widnes and Wakefield, and that they would have been out of their depth in Super League. Others were concerned that the club's successful fund-raising activities had hoovered up all the available money in the town and denied other deserving charities access to potential funds. Mick O'Neill, bitterly disappointed at the failure to progress, contemplated stepping down as chairman. Phil Larder, though, signed a further contract to take him to the end of 1996, while Ian Gately was voted supporters' 'Player of the Year' for the second successive season.

Old Trafford beckons

Meanwhile, there was the small matter of the Premiership. As second division champions, Keighley got two successive home games, beating Hull K.R. 42-16 and London Broncos 38-4, an especially satisfying victory over the team that had been leapfrogged into Super League. Nick Pinkney, with 45 tries in the season, won the Second Division 'Man of Steel' trophy at the end-of-season awards. Simon Irving notched 176 goals and 9 tries - a total of 388 points - in that momentous season.

Now the last drama awaited: an appearance at Old Trafford in the Premiership final. The opponents were Huddersfield, the game played prior to the Wigan-Leeds First Division Final. The players' and directors' wives turned up in two hired American limousines; O'Neill and Smith travelled with Larder and the players on the team coach as usual. Keighley supporters, determined to enjoy this day despite the disappointments of the past few weeks, turned Old Trafford into the Cougar den. They were rewarded with a gritty performance from their heroes, who took time to subdue a determined Huddersfield side, but dominated the second half. Martin Wood was named man-of-the-match, and to cap a great day, Cougar Cubs under-9's beat Underbank 14-6 in a curtain-raiser! It was the club's first trophy in a knock-out competition, and probably the highest point in Keighley's 109-year history. *"The golden age of Keighley rugby league,"* enthused *KN* reporter Keith Reeves. A huge party in Town Hall Square and a civic reception in Bradford followed.

A moment to savour: success at Old Trafford (photo: Graham Smith)

Ian Gately on the charge in the Premiership Final at Old Trafford against Huddersfield (photo: Peter Stell)

Nick Pinkney scores a vital try at Old Trafford (photo: Peter Stell)

Cougar fans take over the Manchester United ground for the day (photo: Brian Lund)

Disappointment at non-promotion didn't dampen ambition at the club, but plans to bring lots of deprived kids from South African townships over for the forthcoming World Cup failed to materialise. Mary Calvert, though, was determined to make contact and forge links with every RL-playing country through the Cougar classroom. The pitch, in a dreadful state at the end of the season and closely resembling a sandpit, still needed drains relaid before being returfed - the work done on it the previous season was apparently a complete waste of money. There were also still plans to build a new stand on the old scrattin' shed side. Then, in early June, came a not entirely unexpected piece of bad news: Magnet, the club's main sponsors for the past four years, were pulling out because of the club's failure to win a Super League place. They did promise, though, to continue to support the Magnet-Whirlpool foundation. On top of this loss of around £40,000, the directors knew that other companies who wanted to come in once the club was in the top division would no longer be interested.

At the same time, Bradford Council refused a cash handout to finance the proposed stand (at the same time denying persistent rumours that payments had secretly been made to Cougars) and Phil Larder wanted a full-time professional playing staff to ensure that Cougars won the promotion place available at the end of the following season. He claims that the directors, who frequently found it difficult to resist anything that would seem to help the club's rise, assured him that sufficient cash would be available to fund what appears in hindsight to have been a very high-risk strategy. The sums had never properly added up, and these equations made it certain that the gap between income and expenditure was going to grow wider. Gary Waller, still very supportive, backed the club's search for a possible cash injection from the Sports Foundation.

Lack of money didn't hold up further signings, this time of richly promising youngsters. Matt Foster and Phil Cantillon were to prove excellent coups for Larder. Cash still dominated the agenda, though. Pinkney and Wood were reported to be holding out for improved contracts, though both eventually signed, Pinkney in a deal that should have kept him at the club until November 1997. By mid-July, all the first-team squad was on board. Keighley were still at odds with the Rugby League over the amount of cash they were to receive from the BSkyB deal - in the end they settled for £500,000 for the first season, much less than even relegated Hull had received. After all the wrangling, though, the club had to pick itself up and start again. The 'quest' was on for Super League.

Another important signing that summer was that of Salford's wing Jason Critchley, who was secured for £55,000 plus a player exchange. Phil Larder had sold Critchley when he was at Widnes, where the player had featured in the second row. Now he realised his mistake and believed Jason to have enormous potential. Larder himself was appointed England coach for the forthcoming World Cup, another bit of prestige for Keighley. Grant Doorey's work with schools continued its impressive march, with 18 teams in the 3rd annual schools RL tournament. Further afield, Keighley were featured in the *Cairns (Queensland) Sunday Mail*, where the club was described as *"ambitious, progressive, zany and wacky"* - and 'Cougarburgers' were mentioned with obvious relish. The Rugby League announced that there would *definitely* be one promotion place from the new First Division to Super League at the end of the first summer season: the target was there to aim for, though some cynics might have felt that if Cougars *did* win it, then some other hoop would have been set up for them to jump through.

Low-key Centenary

Before that, there was the little matter of the Centenary Season to get through. The Rugby League's decision to switch to summer rugby for the start of Super League created the dilemma of a possible ten months without any professional rugby league at all, or the imposition of a meaningless competition to fill in the time before the new structure began. This would mean back-to-back rugby for a whole year. Worse, this hiatus came at the precise time when the game should have been going all-out to publicise and celebrate the centenary of the 1895 breakaway from the Rugby Union. In the event, for many clubs the Centenary Season was a damp squib, a series of games with no meaning played in front of small and often unenthusiastic crowds - though this was not the case at Cougar Park or the grounds that Keighley visited. Overall, there was little celebration of RL's milestone, and it seemed that the game's hierarchy was almost embarrassed by the event, as though they preferred to forget about the past and concentrate on the brave new world to come. As a result, another golden opportunity to promote the game to a wider public was lost as Rugby League played its favourite game, shooting itself in the foot.

Keighley had by now put together a squad that was capable of competing with any Super League club, but was also worth a great deal of money. To O'Neill, they were the

Daryl Powell was Keighley's most expensive signing when he joined them from Sheffield Eagles in April 1995, just days before the announcement of the Rugby Football League's deal with Rupert Murdoch's News Corporation to form the Super League. The fee for Daryl's transfer from Sheffield Eagles was reported to be £130,000, but that gained the Cougars a player of tremendous experience. Daryl had been with the Eagles since the club's formation at the beginning of the 1984/85 season and, whilst playing 312 times for Sheffield, he had also represented England three times and Great Britain 28 times. Powell was signed by Keighley to help clinch promotion to the top flight and to be the key stone of the team at that highest level. He was a natural organiser and leader, and in his position of stand off was able to dictate the pattern of play. His forte was to use his strength to take on the opposition defence, creating space for supporting players to take a well-timed pass and advance towards, if not over, the opposition line. Daryl had won two Divisional Premierships with Sheffield Eagles and made it three with Keighley's 1995 victory. Alas, the record was not maintained as he was in Keighley's losing team of 1996. Daryl became Keighley's second Great Britain international when he toured Papua New-Guinea, Fiji and New Zealand in 1996, making five international appearances. Daryl Powell made a total of 42 appearances for the Cougars and ended his Keighley career as player-coach, before moving on to Leeds Rhinos towards the end of the 1997 season.

Jason Ramshaw was born on 23rd July 1969 at Featherstone and played with Travellers Saints and Lock Lane, where he captained Yorkshire Under 19s and also represented Great Britain Under 19s against New Zealand and France. He played for four seasons with Halifax, including their promotion season and their losing Divisional Premiership Final at Old Trafford in 1991. At Halifax he had a good points scoring record, with 31 tries and 5 drop goals in a total of 75 appearances. Jason joined Keighley on 27th July 1992, making his debut in the first match of the season at home to Workington. He was one of the stalwarts of the successful Cougar era, making the hooking role his own for almost six seasons. He was one of the best all-round players ever to wear a Keighley shirt, having an eye for an opening and a decent burst of speed. He was also a reliable and effective tackler and, from the acting half-back position, was able to manufacture many try scoring opportunities. One of Jason's specialities was, when tackled near the try line, to kick the ball forward, his speed of thought and action outwitting the defence and beating them to the touch down. When the laws were changed to prevent the ball being played forward, Jason was just as effective diving through the defence from the acting half-back position. He was also a useful match winner with his boot, kicking 13 drop goals for the team including a record equalling three in a match against Barrow in the 1993/94 season. He also scored 54 tries for the club in 147 appearances up to the end of the 1997 season. Like many other Keighley players, Jason Ramshaw earned himself two Championship winning medals and two Divisional Premiership Final appearances. In the latter stages of the 1997 season and occasionally prior to that, Jason was given the captaincy of the team, a role for which he was perfectly suited.

club's assets, a team that was already worth much, much more than it had cost to assemble. *'Buying cheap, planning for the future'* was his credo. Daryl Powell was the exception, an expensive buy. But he was brought in to solve a specific problem at stand-off, to further raise the club's profile, and to help Cougars with what was anticipated as a leap to the top flight.

The Centenary Season 1995-96

Apart from a successful trip to a sevens competition at Wigan, where they narrowly lost to the hosts in the semi-final, Keighley began this last (?) winter season against the same opponents they'd met in the previous game, Huddersfield. This time it was at the splendid McAlpine stadium (much better two years later now all four sides are enclosed) in front of a healthy crowd of 4,739, mostly from Keighley. The 36-26 win was followed by a big success at Rochdale, before the first home match of the season, when special entertainment, including a local rock band, was laid on for the visit of Hull. A crowd of over 4,000 was perhaps most surprised by the fact that the pitch had grass on it! The club's first home victory against Hull for 22 years was the icing on the cake. Four more straight wins followed, including, most impressively, a 22-14 success at Salford, who were thought to be Keighley's main rivals in the race for promotion the following summer. Ex-Salford player Critchley was targeted and went off injured, as happened when Salford came to Cougar Park in the first summer season. That victory needed savouring, though: the next four games against Salford were not to be quite so uplifting. The club had three representatives in the World Cup squads: Pinkney and Powell in the English one, Cochrane in the Welsh. Meanwhile, Cougars had still not found a main sponsor to replace Magnet, and when the World Cup did come around, the break in home games helped to trigger yet another of the regular cash crises. The playing successes of September, though, won Cougars the Stones Bitter 'team of the month' award.

The first point of the season was dropped at Widnes on 1st October, but Phil Larder praised the side for its *"superb discipline in a very physical match."* The crowd of 5,496 was typical of the games Keighley were involved in during the Centenary season. Where most clubs saw attendances falling away, figures went up at Cougar Park and away games provided a big boost to clubs involved.

Keighley's contribution to Rugby League had been acknowledged by the granting of a World Cup game. Fiji and South Africa drew nearly 5,000, who were richly entertained by the Fijians' play - as well as their pre-match dancers and vociferous supporters. South Africa were perhaps not good enough to really compete, but played a part in a great occasion. The England squad dropped in at Cougar Park and met a delighted group of youngsters from St. Anne's School, and Larder used the Keighley players in training sessions with the international team. The usual coach convoy to Wembley for the final was organised by Mary Calvert, with 1,000 children on 20 coaches, each staffed by six adults and usually with a Cougar player on board, too.

League action was postponed for the duration of the Centenary World Cup, but there was no shortage of activity behind the scenes - unfortunately, with the wrong kind of public relations message. In mid-October former director Trevor Hobson, who had resigned with chairman Ian Mahady during the great boardroom battle of November 1993, threatened to issue a winding-up order against the Keighley Cougars RLFC Ltd over alleged debts of £12,000 owed to him. As usual, a compromise was reached, but Mahady waded in with a letter to the KN in which he sought to re-iterate the factors that had led him to resign. He explained that he had found it impossible to control the *"excessive spending by Smith and O'Neill."* The team was great, the Cougar classroom was great, but *"none of these things will survive if the company running the Cougars is destroyed. The public should be told the truth about the club's financial position."* Of course, it wasn't, for it is not the way of football or rugby club directors to discuss money matters in public, and fans had to guess what was going on through what they read in the press. One of the main criticisms of Cougars supporters is that they were really left in the dark about so much that was happening during the good playing times and financial crises of the nineties. Mahady's warning proved to be correct. Within 20 months the bubble had burst, the team had fragmented, and the community programme disappeared.

At the end of October, however, another good fairy appeared to rescue the situation. Sponsorless since the withdrawal of Magnet, Cougars found their latest saviour in the shape of Howard Carter, whose local Carta Sports company was booming, and the boss wanted to share the success of his prosperous business. A committed Christian, he said his decision to sponsor Cougars was *"an emotional, prayerful one."* With this latest bit of good news, the local paper urged present and former directors to stop sniping at each other. If only!

Lap of honour at Spotland after clinching the Second Division Championship in 1995

(all photos on this page: Peter Stell)

Celebration time at Cougar Park after the Highfield game

Below: Simon Irving with the trophy

Below right: Popular prop Brendan Hill in 1993

League action resumed with excellent wins at Batley and at home to Featherstone, but there was a big let-down in the first round of the Regal Trophy. Drawn at home against St. Helens in a tie that was selected for BBC TV coverage, expectation was rife that Cougars could spring an upset in front of millions of television viewers. Unfortunately, neither the day nor the players delivered the goods. The weather was atrocious, Saints were beginning to peak as the best club side in the country, and Cougars slid to a dismal 14-42 defeat in front of a meagre crowd of 3,737. Larder classed it as *"the worst performance of the season"* and apologised to fans for the let-down. A bigger crowd watched the next home game, when Keith Dixon scored a hat-trick of tries in a big win over Huddersfield, before Cougar supporters filled Dewsbury's new ground to capacity as the side won 28-6. After this the Centenary season went off the rails. The first defeat of the campaign at Wakefield was followed by Salford's revenge at Cougar Park by 34 points to 6, and the loss of table-topping status, before another point was dropped at Whitehaven in a 8-8 draw. Phil Larder began to look around for players to strengthen his squad as a spate of injuries - including the loss of Daryl Powell for the rest of the season with a broken thumb - showed up the lack of reserve strength in his squad. He nevertheless insisted that the spirit among the players was the best he had seen at any club.

Meanwhile, some students from Greenhead Grammar School put Cougars on an Internet site, and Keith Reeves' end of year report for the *KN* hailed 1995 as *"the greatest year in the history of Keighley Rugby League Club. Almost everybody with an interest in sport knew they (Cougars) had arrived - yet officials of the RFL chose to ignore them."* Injuries had underlined the lack of strength in depth, though, and there was no money available to attract any new recruits: the gamble to take the club into full-time professionalism might just be backfiring. 1995 also ended, regrettably, with another winding-up threat from Trevor Hobson, before a £9,000 debt was paid, and a 12-20 reverse at Hull on the last day of the calendar year, ending any remaining championship hopes. The new Turner stand at the bottom of the ground was scheduled to be opened at the Boxing Day game, but bad weather caused its postponement, and the ceremony took place on January 7th before a low crowd of 2,262 at the Rochdale game, which was thankfully won.

The signing of Wesley Berry was a scoop - or two - but it didn't work out for the Cougars

One of the more bizarre Cougar stories surfaced early in the new year, when it was announced that a gentleman with the tantalising name of Wesley 'Two Scoops' Berry had signed. This American apparently ran fast, lifted weights to excess, appeared on *Gladiators*, and jumped over cars as a hobby. But could he play rugby? Wesley never had, but he turned out for the 'A' team and said he enjoyed himself. What might have turned into an interesting story to watch, however, evaporated when the Rugby League announced new regulations on the number of overseas players, and Wesley had to depart.

Both the last two home games of the Centenary season attracted 3,500+ crowds; a narrow defeat to Widnes was followed by a 14-8 victory over Batley, a result which clinched runners-up spot. The campaign ended with a 14-30 loss at Featherstone. All that was left in the winter now was the Challenge Cup, which has been stranded in pre-Super League season instead of being a climax. In 1996 it was sandwiched in between the rolling programme. Keighley, with a continuing injury crisis, just beat Barrow in the first round, but were then soundly thrashed at Hull 12-42. Few Keighley supporters travelled to this one. Larder reaffirmed his commitment to the squad that had performed so well in the first half of the season, though one major signing of the short close season was Sheffield's Sonny Whakarau, who arrived in February. Now the priority for the first summer campaign was lots of season ticket sales.

Good Cougar news included the re-appointment of Phil Larder as Great Britain coach and the inclusion of five players in the squads for the World 'Nines' tournament: Wood, Pinkney and Cantillon in the England squad, Cochrane and Critchley for Wales.

The Quest for Super League

Less than a year on from rejection for the top flight, the whole focus now was to win the restyled First Division and secure a Super League spot. The early signs were auspicious: 4,700 came along on March 31st 1996 to see Dewsbury demolished 54-2 in the first game, with Daryl Powell man-of-the-match. The gates at Cougar Park opened at 12.30 and pre-match entertainment featured an Academy game and Gwen and Andy, a duo who sang and encouraged fans to feel involved in the occasion - as if anyone needed any second invitation! The matchday programme included plenty of upbeat comment, with both Mick O'Neill and newly-appointed chief executive Kevan Halliday-Brown hailing the coming season as *"the most important in the club's history."* Halliday-Brown was brought in as chief executive after a high profile advertising campaign which the directors felt necessary to remind RL headquarters at Red Hall (it moved there from Chapeltown Road in the same city of Leeds in 1994) that Keighley were serious about admission to Super League. He stayed with the club until September 1997, but never established himself as an independent decision-maker who could tackle the horrendous underlying financial problems. Phil Larder, while bemoaning the decision that saw Keighley excluded from Super League, pointed out that *"we now have to get on with our life. We must look forward and aim to be champions this season."* More good news followed during the week, with a 'mystery consortium' pumping a reputed £150,000 into the club, and the signing of two young Australian stars, Andy King and Steve Parsons. Things continued to go well on the field, and by the end of May Cougars had won seven and drawn one of their first eight games. The competitive standard in the division was emphasised by the tightness of four of those matches: two-point wins at Rochdale and Huddersfield, a 34-30 victory over Hull at home, and a 22-22 draw against Featherstone at Cougar Park. Attendances were still improving, though, with over 6,000 for the Hull game and over 5,000 for the visit of Featherstone. Cougars' pre-match entertainment for the summer games was proving to be an important overall part of the scene, and the half-time 'stand-up' bingo that Mick O'Neill introduced was both a useful money-spinner and good fun. In a reverse of the normal rules, fans with cards were encouraged to walk on the pitch towards the main stand, staying in the game as long as none of their numbers were read out. The effect of a hopeful competitor having to turn round at the last minute in a friendly humiliation added to the good-humoured atmosphere of the day. Mascot Freddy Cougar circled round and round the ground during the afternoon, shaking hands with everyone and providing a fun focus. And, of course, there was always Mick on the microphone, pumping up the tempo with lively banter and a suitable record for every home score. It was heady stuff, an irresistable cocktail.

Simon Irving was born in Dewsbury on 22nd March 1967 and played Rugby Union with Cleckheaton and Headingley, representing Yorkshire Colts, Yorkshire Under 21s and England 'B'. He turned professional with Leeds on 30th January 1990 and played a total of 83 games, notching 23 tries and 235 goals, before joining Keighley on 7th September 1994, making his debut four days later at London Broncos. Simon joined Keighley primarily for his goal kicking skills and, although a centre-threequarter, was not noted for his defensive abilities. That side of his game, though, improved tremendously and by the time he rejoined Leeds, during the 1997 season, he was one of the best tacklers in the squad. He formed a potent attacking force with fellow centre Nick Pinkney and created many scoring opportunities for his colleagues. In almost four seasons with Keighley, Simon was the main goal kicker, although injury did restrict his appearances, and consequently, his points tally. His 824 points came from 46 tries and 320 goals in 83 appearances for the club, his best season being the 2nd Division Championship and Divisional Premiership winning season of 1994/95 when he contributed 22 tries and 152 goals.

> *Team for the first summer season game was: Stoop; Eyres, Pinkney, Irving, Critchley; Powell, Robinson; Gately, Ramshaw, Doorey, Fleary, Larder, Wood.*

A big win at Batley marked the return of prop Steve Hall sixteen months after breaking his leg. Injuries to other players were beginning to take their toll, though. With Keighley and Salford neck and neck at the top of the league, the visit of the Reds on the first Sunday in June not surprisingly attracted a near-capacity attendance of 6,564. Unfortunately, on a beautiful day that was tailor-made for summer rugby, the game was a terrible disappointment for home fans. Jason Critchley was taken out in an off-the-ball incident after less than a minute, and a strong Salford side totally imposed itself on the Cougars, putting the game beyond reach by half-time. Martin Wood scored Keighley's only try in a 8-45 defeat. Worse, play had to be held up after a crash barrier collapsed at the Lawkholme Lane end, putting a question mark over the club's ability to accommodate a full house. The plot was revived with a 12-6 win at Widnes, but a week later, defeat at Dewsbury seemed to signal the end of Super League ambitions. Five points had been dropped already, and Salford had a look of invincibility. At the end of June, Rochdale were comprehensively beaten 42-12 at Cougar Park, with Nick Pinkney getting a hat-trick, and then there was a marvellous 26-14 success at The Boulevard against Hull.

Pinkney scored his 100th try for Keighley, and Martin Wood had what was probably his best game for the club so far. Behind the scenes, though, yet another series of bombshells was about to explode. The finances were out of control yet again, and the huge wage bill necessitated by the full-time squad was proving a massive drain. The mystery 'business consortium' which had been brought on board during March in a somewhat secretive manner was apparently propping up the club's current expenses rather than injecting investment cash. Even so, by the end of June, the financial problems were horrendous: there was no money to pay wages, and the club appeared close to collapse. In early July, the head of the 'mystery' group, which was now prepared to put even more money into the club, was revealed as Carl Metcalfe, a local millionaire with a business background that was not entirely clearly documented. In fact, rumours soon began spreading around Keighley that Metcalfe was connected with the supply of illicit drugs. This he vigorously and immediately denied: *"I am not and never have been involved with drugs,"* he told the *Keighley News*.

Nevertheless, a week before the announcement of his involvement with Cougars, Mary Calvert, who had spearheaded the club's anti-drugs campaign and won national praise for it, resigned *"for personal reasons."* Less than a month later, she was appointed Drugs Services Co-ordinator in the town, totally independent of the rugby club. At the same time, the police, schools, volunteers, and the *KN* launched a new anti-drugs awareness campaign.

The local paper paid fulsome tribute to Mary Calvert for fighting *"this evil in our midst...the anti-drugs work which has been carried out through the Keighley Cougar classroom has brought great honour to the town and the club."*

It was also the end of the road for Mick O'Neill. Unable to raise any more cash to meet the running costs of the Cougars, he was forced to leave the board, along with Neil Spencer and Maurice Barker (though Mike Smith remained), to make way for the new directors demanded by the business consortium. *"Radio Mike goes off air,"* proclaimed the local paper, and indeed it would after one more announcement the following Sunday. Reporter Keith Reeves was in no doubt as to the O'Neill effect on Keighley Cougars: *"Never mind raising the club profile, he has propelled it forward a hundred years."* Bradford Bulls chairman Chris Caisley eulogised: *"Mick's enthusiasm and vision have played a significant part in the development of the Cougars; without him, they could not have succeeded in capturing the imagination of the Keighley public in the way they have."* O'Neill is adamant that plans were already in hand to ensure Keighley's ongoing progress: a new cantilever stand was being projected for the uncovered side, and, importantly, he was negotiating with the Co-op to buy back the ground.

Mick O'Neill had been the highly public face of Keighley Cougars, though the other two directors who resigned at the same time had been equally dedicated to the club and put in much time and money. Maurice Barker, for example, had revamped one of the bars at his own expense.

O'Neill was devastated at having to leave, and continued to campaign against the new management, attempting on several occasions to raise the money to get back onto the board. He felt a heavy personal responsibility for what he saw as a failure, and was reluctant even to go out socially in Keighley for a long time. When he eventually did begin to venture out again, he was amazed at the warmth and affection for him among Cougars supporters. Almost two years later, he still cannot go and watch, but has no regrets about being involved. *"I'm glad I did it,"* he says. So, too, are thousands of fans.

The programme for the Huddersfield game carried no hint that anything was amiss, but at half-time O'Neill came onto the pitch - scene of those momentous announcements at the time of Super League launch - and bid an emotional farewell to the fans. His own particular dream died that afternoon. The fact that Huddersfield gave the team a 37-10 drubbing, and that there were more injuries to add to a growing list made the day even less palatable for the Cougars supporters in an excellent 5,427 crowd.

Though Metcalfe's arrival was not officially announced until early July 1996, he and his associates had in fact been propping up the club since the second game of the season. By mid-March, after an abbreviated Centenary Season and a few cup games, the directors and sponsors had put in as much money as they could afford. Both O'Neill and Smith knew the writing was on the wall. The introduction of someone who was prepared to put up the money to apparently save the club seemed too good to be true. Carl Metcalfe, an ostentatiously wealthy man, came in as chairman with a bang, announcing plans to develop Cougar Park into a multi-million pound entertainment complex. The ground capacity would be increased to 12,000 under a three-year 'Cougar 2000' plan evoking the concept of Nov Camp in Barcelona, and a marketing company would be set up in town to promote the club. Metcalfe said he aimed to model himself on Blackburn Rovers' chairman Jack Walker, and also promised to seek an early meeting with RL chief Maurice Lindsay, who he described as a *"truly visionary leader."* It would have been difficult to find many people in Keighley who would have agreed with that particular description. Metcalfe was optimistic, though, that Keighley would still be in a position to join Super League if they could finish in second position and SL was expanded, as seemed possible. *"Don't ask me about rugby, though,"* he told reporters, referring them to coach Phil Larder on questions regarding that topic. He did, however, bring some financial reality to a set-up that had feasted on success without always balancing the cost.

The massive wage bill was rapidly identified as the main cost-cutting measure by the new administration, which claimed to have inherited a far worse financial situation than had been revealed. Metcalfe was later to say that if he had known the full extent of the club's debts, he would never have got involved. The first victim of cost-cutting measures - apparently - was Phil Larder (though the team's poor performance against Huddersfield, and Larder's dual role as Great Britain coach were cited as the ostensible reasons), who was told at the end of July that his contract would not be renewed after the end of the season. The club would have preferred he kept quiet, but Larder immediately went public. *"I feel like I have been kicked in the guts,"* he said, but vowed to take the team to second place in the division and win the end-of-season premiership. *"We have done too much, enjoyed too much success, earned too much respect, to throw it all away. I also have too much pride."* The fans' verdict on Larder was apparent from the sustained applause he received whenever he appeared at the start of a game, or walked across the pitch at Keighley to his preferred vantage point opposite the main stand. Letters expressing shock and horror poured into the *KN*. *"Like shooting ourselves through the heart...worst mistake since Terry Hollindrake sold to Hull...dispensing with the services of the best coach in modern times,"* were typical comments.

Phil Larder's contribution to Keighley was undoubtedly immense; a thoroughly professional, modern coach, who used every bit of technical assistance and analysis to help him understand and prepare his players, he also made big demands on them, and expected total commitment from a squad that he himself had wanted to be full-time. Despite the disappointment over the way it ended, Larder is adamant that his time at Keighley was his most enjoyable time in sport. *"I loved every minute of it."* Highlights for him were the cup defeat of Sheffield Eagles, and the narrow loss to Warrington - *"I knew we were on the right track then."* Then, of course, there was the Premiership win. He is glowing in his praise of the Keighley supporters, and rated enormously the players he worked with at Keighley. Among the best were Andre Stoop - *"exciting"*, Simon Irving - *"rock solid"*, Chris Robinson - *"a great organiser"*, and Darren Fleary - *"outstanding."* Larder knew, though, that if the team didn't make Super League in 1996, his contract would be unlikely to be renewed.

Rumours that some of the players would leave soon became rife; Martin Wood was transfer-listed at his own request; and Powell and Irving turned down an offer of the coaching job.

The rugby perked up after this. An 18-18 draw at Whitehaven after a woeful first-half performance brought a point to be thankful for, before superb wins at Featherstone (48-20, with Keith Dixon getting his 1,000th point for the club) and at home to Wakefield Trinity by 46-14 in front of a respectable 4,789 crowd. Australian centre Andy King, a recent recruit, scored seven tries in these two games, as Keighley's roller-coaster season took a turn for the better. Daryl Powell was outstanding and hugely influential in both these games. A presentation of a decanter to Keith Dixon before the Wakefield game was made by chairman Metcalfe, whose mind was on securing entry to Super League by some means or other. Negotiations with Maurice Lindsay were apparently foundering on the unsuitability of Cougar Park to house big games. The original criteria demanded a 10,000 capacity, with seating for 2,500, and at least 6,000 spectators under cover. The idea of ground-sharing with Burnley Football Club at Turf Moor was mooted, to which Lindsay is supposed to have given his backing, though he says: *"I always made it clear that any decision to move was in the hands of Keighley and its supporters."* Metcalfe proclaimed *"I am 95% certain we can get in."* Move to Burnley? Most people were horrified at the idea, which seemed at a stroke to render pointless the idea of having a town rugby team at all. How could a side calling itself Keighley play 20 miles away - and in *Lancashire* of all places! It made about as much sense as a football club called Brighton playing in Kent, or Wimbledon transferring to Dublin. One of those has happened, and the other has been seriously suggested, but both negate the whole point of having a community team. The *Keighley News* was in no doubt. *"The whole phenomenon surrounding Keighley Cougars is much more than rugby league. It is about hope. It is about this town and its image. The Cougars are an inviolable part of Keighley."* MP Gary Waller launched a campaign to keep the Cougars in Keighley: *"Nobody should be in any doubt that the Cougars as a*

Above: Grant Doorey - a massive performance on the field and in the community. Above right: Darren Fleary - gave fans top value. Below right: Andy Eyres, another player who became heavily involved in the club's work in the community (photos: Peter Stell)

Below: young fans watch Chris Robinson take a conversion (photo: Brian Lund)

present day phenomenon depend on the loyalty of the fans who have followed the team through thick and thin....it is inconceivable their home could be anywhere else." Fans, too, were saying in no uncertain terms that they wouldn't travel to Burnley, and made it clear that they preferred the First Division if the price of Super League was having to move. Metcalfe seemed captivated by the Holy Grail, and wrote a strong defence of the planned move in the programme for the game against Widnes on August 18th. He also repeated the fact that without him the club would have gone bankrupt soon after the season began. *"We need Super League, or we close and start again... the choice is yours."* Indeed, supporters were presented with a voting slip in the programme, but the questions were weighted in such a fashion that unsurprisingly, a majority of those responding chose the option *'move to Burnley temporarily until Cougar Park is developed.'* It was hardly a ringing endorsement.

Keighley had lost to Salford at the Willows the previous week in a game in which Salford clinched top spot and the one guaranteed Super League place. Back at Cougar Park, though, Cougars demolished Widnes 64-12 and then beat Batley 40-14 to secure second place, and keep alive faint hopes that, if the rules should be changed, they might slip in. Would SL be enlarged to 13 or 14 clubs? It was not to be. The Rugby Football League's track record in consistency was not unblemished, but on this occasion it remained straight down the line. No entry for Keighley - at Cougar Park or Burnley. If Keighley had arranged to play all their home games at Wembley, some other objection would have been raised.

Those last two home games in the summer of 1996 were something special, however. Against Widnes, Jason Critchley smashed a 92-year old club record as he scored six tries. Ike Jagger's 1906 feat had been equalled three times since - twice by Nick Pinkney - but the Critchley performance was tremendous. *"For the first 20 minutes, we were almost perfect!"* enthused the soon-to-depart Phil Larder. The Batley game marked the first team debut of Marlon Billy, a speedy young winger who looked like a potential Martin Offiah and scored two tries.

All that remained now were the Premiership play-offs. Larder would obviously have preferred to leave with another win at Old Trafford. The semi-final - at home to Hull - was certainly memorable. An England v. South African students curtain-raiser and the appearance of the pop group Black Lace provided pre-match entertainment, and Cougars, in a wonderful first half performance, raced to a 28-0 lead. Unfortunately, one of the five tries, scored by Keith Dixon under the noses of Hull supporters in the Turner stand, and awarded by referee Steve Presley after consulting his touch judges, was sufficiently controversial to spark a crowd disturbance. Protesting visiting fans spilled onto the pitch, and two arrests had to be made before some sort of order was restored after 20 minutes. Meanwhile, the teams had left the field until things quietened down. This sort of occurrence is rare in rugby league, which has always prided itself on the friendly attitude and relations between opposing fans, who normally co-habit on the terraces without problems. It was not good public relations for Keighley, whose ground had been one of the main levers used to prohibit SL entry. After the interval, Hull fought back, and an entertaining contest finished with Keighley winning 41-28. Daryl Powell, who had been playing superbly in recent weeks, was man-of-the-match with a display of genius and flair. The Cougars' second successive visit to a final didn't end so happily, however. Salford beat them for the third time that season 21-6 in a tight, old-fashioned game in which the Radio 5 commentary team felt they had not had the rub of the referee's decisions. Cantillon, Fleary and Whakarau had top games. Some kind of revenge was gained a week later, when the Academy side beat Salford 31-25 at Cougar Park in their cup competition.

Five days later, it was confirmed that Keighley were not to be fast-tracked into Super League, which was to stay at 12 teams. Talk of moving to Burnley had subsided and was now dead; it is doubtful if serious negotiations had ever been set in motion (Mike Smith claims it was all a bluff to dissuade the Rugby League Council from fast-tracking any other club - if this is the case, it upset a lot of people unnecessarily) but local hostility ensured the plan was effectively negated. Plans were still being mooted to develop Cougar Park, though, especially with an anticipated £600,000 due to arrive from the Murdoch sponsorship for the following season. Phil Larder said his farewells - *"we've had something very special..."* and Powell and Irving were confirmed as joint coaches. During the initial furore after the news broke that Larder would be leaving, football director Allan Clarkson, an ex-Keighley player and crowd favourite, was at pains to point out that the club was looking for another top coach, and that interest in the coaching job had been shown *"from all over the world."* The name of the Wigan scrum-half Shaun Edwards was even leaked to the press. But it is inconceivable that Keighley, who were seeking to control and trim their wage bill, would have brought in another big name. In any case, who was better than Larder anyway? The two respected players who were to take over aimed to keep the existing squad together; this was always going to be an impossible ambition.

Critchley and Powell were selected to go to Papua/ New Guinea and New Zealand on what was to be an ill-fated Great Britain tour. While away they encountered riots and shootings in PNG, and the tour ended in fiasco as RL headquarters hauled back eleven of the players towards the end to save money. When he came back, Daryl Powell launched a blistering attack on the administration of the tour and announced his retirement from international rugby. Powell was still away, though, when the Cougar financial bubble finally burst, and the board, despairing of mounting costs and uncontrollable debts, decided to put the club into administration. Carl Metcalfe had continued to put money in to pay wages and general running expenses, but by now he'd had enough. In October 1996, Keighley RLFC had debts of over a million pounds, owed mainly to the Inland Revenue, various breweries and former and current directors. Calling in an administrator would freeze and ring-fence those debts until the club's affairs could be stabilised.

The man who was charged with setting the business on the right road was Peter O'Hara, who was to stay at Keighley for over 14 months. He had the power to hire and fire directors and organise repayment plans with those individuals and organisations owed money: a creditors' voluntary agreement. Mike Smith said persuasively that the move would safeguard the club for the town, and that it would eventually put Cougars on a firm financial footing. Corrective action now would make the club stronger in future. It was obvious, though, that the majority of players would have to lose their full-time status. Perhaps it wasn't quite appreciated just how savage the culling would have to be in the coming months. In retrospect, the decision to make the whole squad full-time in 1995 had to be seen as a gamble which backfired: its viability could only have been made possible by winning promotion in the first summer season. When that didn't happen, there was no way that Keighley could justify the policy.

The first player casualties included Andy King and Steve Parsons, the recent arrivals from Australia, old favourite Brendan Hill, and the promising youngster Gareth Cochrane. Daryl Powell, in New Zealand, took the news philosophically. Maurice Lindsay, in a meeting with the administrator, had apparently demanded the resignation of Smith and Clarkson as the price for the Rugby League Council's acquiescence in what was going on. This was resisted by Metcalfe, who provided a four-point pledge for supporters: the team would not be weakened by what was going on, the coaches would remain, Cougar Park would be full for a friendly game on New Year's Day, and the team would win Division One in 1997. The first of these was unsustainable, the third unlikely, and the fourth surely out of reach.

Promising winger Marlon Billy was signed on a contract, but sponsored by International Boulevard Hair Salon, run by the chairman's daughter, as the club itself was not allowed to invest in any new players or take on further commitments while in administration. On the debit side, Andre Stoop left to return to South Africa.

In the event, the game scheduled for January 1st was postponed for four days because the terraces were frozen and unsafe. When it took place, 2,589 watched Cougars lose to Huddersfield 16-25 after dominating the first half. On Boxing Day, the first of a holiday double-header against the same club had Keighley losing 10-40 at the McAlpine

Cougar Spice are now a familiar part of the pre-match entertainment at Keighley (photo: Brian Lund)

Marlon Billy builds up speed in a game against Leigh in 1997 (photo: Brian Lund)

Martin Wood - hugely influential during his time at Cougar Park (photo: Peter Stell)

The clock and scoreboard - almost the only things that didn't change at Cougar Park (photo: Brian Lund)

Stadium. It has to be said that at this stage Cougars looked nothing like promotion challengers.

Five days later, a creditor's meeting gave the administrator eight weeks to sort out a workable plan for paying off debts. His work was not helped by the late arrival of Sky TV money from RL headquarters. Peter O'Hara was determined to make progress and turn the club around, but was in no mood to mince his words. *"If it (the club) is to go forward, it cannot be run like an amateur bowling club. It must have a strong financial manager, and be run like a business, not a hobby ruled by petty jealousies."* The implication was clear that if O'Hara could not find a viable solution, the club could fold.

Transfers were inevitable, and it was a blow, but not a surprise, when Sheffield Eagles showed interest in two of Keighley's best players, Nick Pinkney and Martin Wood. Sheffield had snapped up Phil Larder when he became available (but, curiously, did not retain him for long) and Larder was bound to look at the top players with whom he'd worked at Cougar Park. Keighley netted a welcome £95,000 plus utility back Mark Gamson from the deal. Two players came on free transfers from Halifax - Ian St. John Ellis, the talented but temperamental ex-Castleford player, and Lafaele Filipo, and chairman Metcalfe felt the need to be positive: *"The club will go from strength to strength...prospects have never looked so good."* That might not have been enough to convince the fans.

The first round of the 1997 Challenge Cup did end happily, in a 62-4 win. But this was against amateur team Redhill. The real test was yet to come. February was a marvellous month, though, underlining the constant ability of the Keighley team and management to pull out all the stops when the situation looked bleakest. The Cougar classroom was re-instated, under the charge of Grant Doorey, who was also looking after the local schools rugby tournament. The team performed well in the Joe Phillips Trophy game at Odsal, losing 20-36 to Super League outfit Bradford Bulls in front of a crowd of 7,700 but playing with flair and providing lots of entertainment. This was a revival of the traditional pre-season friendly not played since 1994.

1997 - another chance

Director Mike Smith now asked for fresh ideas to take the Cougars to new heights. Whatever the situation, the mood was positive. The optimism was matched by performances on the field, with two tremendous wins in the Challenge Cup, both away from home. First, the long trip to Workington to play the side relegated from Super League ended with a 24-14 win and magnificent performances from Powell and Steve Hall, deservedly man of the match. The same two were again outstanding a week later when Cougars took on Super League side Halifax and outscored them by three tries (by Filipo, Foster and Irving) to one, 21-8, before a 7,421 crowd. Larder's assertion that Keighley would have done well if promoted was fully justified by these two performances. In early March, more good news: the creditors approved a rescue plan put forward by O'Hara. On March 2nd, the first league game at Whitehaven was won 22-10, with Chris Robinson man-of-the-match.

The Cup successes set up a quarter-final meeting with St. Helens at Cougar Park. Saints had won both the inaugural Super League as well as the Challenge Cup the previous season and were arguably the best side in the country. It was yet another wonderful occasion for Keighley, another big-time set-piece. The game was an all-ticket sell-out with a capacity crowd of 7,845, and as ever at such times, a superb atmosphere was generated at the homely ground, with the crowd close to the action on all four sides. The game itself was exciting and awe-inspiring without ever holding out much prospect of Keighley winning. St Helens were without their suspended captain Bobbie Goulding, but still had too much fire-power. That Cougars restricted them to four tries spoke volumes for their gutsy performance. The large crowd caused a problem at half-time, however, when Saints fans attempted to move from the Turner Stand to Spion Kop at the other end. This traditional custom works well at most grounds with less dense crowds, but on this occasion was totally inappropriate, as there was just no room for anyone to get through. The public address system, too late, enjoined fans to stay where they were, but it would have been better if police and stewards had been alert to the situation and been present at the Turner end in some effective numbers. In the event, everything was sorted fairly amicably, but half-time lasted 35 minutes.

The following week sunk Keighley's season almost before it had started. The Rugby League decided that the club should play its home league match against Hull, postponed because of the St Helens cup game, on the Wednesday, just three days later. On top of that, the match scheduled for the following weekend was away to Huddersfield. These two teams were likely to be Cougars' main rivals in the promotion race, and playing three pressure games in eight days was not ideal, especially with three key players injured after the Saints game. In the event, a team still exhausted from the Sunday cup game went down 8-13 to Hull, and was beaten heavily at the McAlpine stadium by 36 points to 12. That latter game was out of reach after Huddersfield's rampaging first twenty minutes had taken them to a winning lead. To make matters worse, Steve Hall suffered yet another injury.

The league season stuttered for another month. A 34-12 victory at Swinton included 18 points from Simon Irving, and a top performance from Jason Ramshaw. Ironically, Swinton had sacked their coach Peter Roe, the man well-known to Keighley fans, just 24 hours before the game. Then came a shock 12-21 defeat at home to Whitehaven, with the team a shadow of their former selves. A visit to Hull Kingston Rovers scooped one league point in a 22-22 draw after Keighley let a 12-point lead slip, before a huge home win against Widnes. The margin was 56-2, but the crowd for the midweek evening game an ominously small 1,605. Four days later came the most disappointing performance of the season, a 16-26 reverse at home to Dewsbury, the club that so often seemed to have spiked Cougars' ambitions.

These inconsistent performances were bound to have off-field repercussions. Still trying to trim the wage bill, Keighley first gave Keith Dixon a free transfer and cancelled Latham Tawhai's contract. Dixon was one of the club's longest-serving players, and was obviously disappointed that his career at the club had ended this way. After the Dewsbury game, though, things took off. Powell was absolutely furious with the display, and the directors decided to act: all but six players were put on the transfer list to slice a huge amount off the wage bill. Full-time players were a luxury the club was not able to afford now. The Super League dream was in tatters.

Playing performances improved after this. Critchley and St John Ellis (in his penultimate game for Keighley) scored hat-tricks in a 42-22 win at Wakefield, before the team, back to something like its best, beat Huddersfield 18-12 at home to climb into third spot in the First Division. While Hull and Huddersfield were well out of sight at the top of the table, with the former installed as hot favourites for the promotion spot, it was important that Cougars finished as high in the league as possible to secure a higher payment from the BSkyB sponsorship money. A trip to the Boulevard saw a top performance, though Keighley lost by the odd point in 25. A home win against Workington, with scrum-half Chris Robinson in top form, was followed by defeat at bottom club Widnes. *"The first 40 minutes were the worst I have seen from a Keighley side,"* said Powell. The team was slowly changing, and young players such as Rob Roberts and Paul Owen were beginning to make their mark. The next three games were won, including a crucial one at Whitehaven, who were also challenging for third spot. Paying the players suddenly became a problem again; less than half the anticipated monthly payment from the News Corporation sponsorship appeared on the basis that the Rugby League felt it unlikely that Keighley would finish in the top three. Prize money for the First Division varied from two to six hundred thousand pounds, depending on where a club finished at the end of the season. This put more pressure on the current account, and wage payments had to be delayed until gate receipts had been counted from the home game against Hull Kingston Rovers at the end of June, when newcomer Adrian Flynn (ex-Castleford) and stalwart Darren Fleary had excellent games in a 12-4 success. Flynn somewhat blotted his copybook when he was sent off in the first minute of the next match at - where else? - Dewsbury, which Cougars predictably lost 14-19.

Sale of the Century

The following Wednesday Keighley once again made the national sporting pages, though not for reasons that the town would have wished. *"Leeds in bargain deal,"* was the *Guardian*'s rather understated headline over a story which broke the news that nine of Keighley's best players had been snapped up by the Super League team Leeds Rhinos for a seemingly derisory £25,000. *"Rhinos rescue threatened Cougars,"* announced the *Yorkshire Post*. The *Keighley News* weighed in with *"Sale of the Century."* On the face of it, that seemed pretty accurate: nine players (Powell, Irving, Cantillon, Roberts, Flynn, Foster, Fleary, Robinson, and David Larder, son of ex-coach Phil) were to go for the price of a four-wheel drive, and it appeared that the Keighley team had been scooped up by a predatory neighbour whose chief executive Gary Hetherington was probably viewed by Keighley folk in a similar light to the Rugby League's supremo. But the deal, and the situation that provoked it, was much more complicated. Administrator Peter O'Hara was making little headway in the battle to balance the books, mainly because of the huge player wage bill, and he eventually decided that this draconian move was the only way to save the club. Keighley director Allan Clarkson explained that it was a good deal: Leeds were prepared to take over the contract payments for these nine players, would lend six of them back to Cougars until the end of the current season and the subsequent Premiership games, and there was the prospect of further payments to Cougars if any of the players were sold on to another club. Further, there was the possibility of a 'buy-back' in the future. The 'transfer' fee had already been used - paying the wages of the backroom staff the previous week. Main sponsor Howard Carter called it *"a brilliant deal,"* and O'Hara said it was the last chance of survival for the stricken club. Supporters, watching the bulk of their favourite players disappear, were not so sanguine. *"Just what is happening at the Cougars?"* wrote an irate fan to the KN. *"Soon there will be nothing left....where are the 'millions' that were promised a few months ago? Hollow promises!"* Former chairman Mick O'Neill and the *Keighley News* itself were hostile to the deal, attributing cynical motives to Hetherington and the Rhinos. All the officials at Cougar Park claimed that the arrangement was good for the club, but it was very difficult for the average supporter on the terraces for the home game against Wakefield the following Sunday to see much else than an impending slide into oblivion. Leeds coach Dean Bell was in the stand along with Hetherington to have a close look at some of the players his club had just bought, though he may not have been too impressed on the day. In the event, Keighley edged home 20-18 with a last-minute try, and the world didn't seem quite so bad. But, leaving the ground that day, it really did feel like the end of an era.

Carl Metcalfe spelled out the financial realities during the next week. The annual wage bill at the start of the year had been one and a quarter million pounds. The aim was to cut it back to a more manageable £400,000.

The loss of Daryl Powell and Simon Irving seemed a particularly big blow. Against many people's expectations, they had kept the side on track towards the top of the First Division. Both games against Hull, who had clinched top spot, had been very close and might have been won with a little luck. Keighley had beaten Huddersfield, the second-placed team, at Cougar Park, proof that the side could live with the best. Moreover, Powell's own performances during the season had been excellent and inspiring. He had been the epitome of Keighley's new-found status in the rugby league world, the best of the players that had been attracted to Cougar Park, largely through the efforts of Mick O'Neill. When he arrived in 1995, Powell said that he found the prospect of joining Keighley a new challenge at a time when he had been thinking of leaving Sheffield Eagles after being with them since the club's formation in 1984. He had in fact been Gary Hetherington's first signing for the Eagles. Daryl was impressed with the ambitions of the management team at Keighley and the skill level of the players. He found the atmosphere at Cougar Park a huge improvement on the Don Valley stadium, where the crowd is basically on only one side of the pitch. The supporters were *"unique"* in their passion. Powell was signed at the end of the 1994-95 season, with the intention of bolstering the team for success after promotion, but then the Super League bombshell dropped. He was *"devastated"* when Keighley were excluded, as were the other players who had worked so hard to gain access to a higher standard. Nevertheless, Daryl was determined to help the club succeed, described his two years at Keighley as marvellous, and was sad to have to leave - though it was perfectly obvious to everyone that the club could not carry on without some drastic solution to the financial problems. Powell enjoyed, too, his venture into coaching, though he and Simon Irving were catapulted into the job and forced to learn under pressure. Simon tended to concentrate on the administrative side while Daryl did the coaching, but the pair made a great team. He rated the cup win at Halifax in February 1997 as the high point of his coaching career.

During the summer of 1997, Mick O'Neill had made constant attempts to put together a group which could buy back the club from administration, and claims that, although he approached the administrator on several occasions with a solid offer of £250,000, made up of guarantees from five individuals, all his initiatives were rejected. It was planned that John Kain, who had worked under Larder, Powell and Irving, would take over as coach, and Jason Ramshaw was pencilled in as captain for the 1998 season. Irving and Powell made their last appearances - though not as players - in the last game of the season at Post Office Road, Featherstone, where a relaxed Irving spent most of a hot afternoon coming on with the water bottles. *"Has any other club,"* he said later, *"won promotion twice, but found themselves still in the same league the following year?"* The Irving connection at Keighley was not finished, however; after becoming the first player to re-sign for Leeds in that club's 106-year history, he was amazingly back at Cougar Park by the end of the year. When Leeds decided he wouldn't feature in future first team plans, he moved onto Wakefield Rugby Union Club until they, too, ran into a financial quagmire in Autumn 1997. The game against Featherstone was, unfortunately, lost 14-16, but the sizeable contingent of Keighley supporters in the crowd was in upbeat mood about the club's chances for the future. The result still secured Keighley's third place position - for Whitehaven to have overtaken them that day, Cougars would have had to lose heavily, or Whitehaven win by a cricket score. Despite the fact that virtually all the stars who'd contributed to the glory years had left, or were about to go on their way, the Cougar army was convinced that, somehow, things would be okay again. One player who was making his final appearance for Keighley that day was the big-hearted Australian prop Grant Doorey, whose contribution to the Cougar community ideal - as well as his performances on the pitch - had been immense. He went to join French club Villeneuve, who ironically may be playing at Cougar Park in 1998 if a proposed Anglo-French competition goes ahead at the end of the season. Doorey's parting shot to the town was to underline the fact that more sporting facilities were needed for the youngsters in the area. The chairman said that the Cougar classroom would be taken over by Jason Ramshaw.

Meanwhile, two further departures were confirmed: Jason Critchley to Castleford, and Keith Dixon to Dewsbury. Chief executive Kevin Halliday-Brown also said his farewells, but John Kain was in upbeat mood, stating his intention to develop once again the club's links with the community.

Director Mike Smith was told to leave, too, by administrator O'Hara. The club apparently no longer needed a commercial director.

The curtain had come down on the league season, but someone had dreamt up an end-of-term premiership competition which involved up to ten matches. Clubs had complained that the new fixture setup in the summer involved too few games and too short a season: ten home league matches meant gate revenue potential was inadequate. But Keighley were having serious reservations about taking part in the premiership at all because it seemed that winning pay of £300 would not be offset by what were expected to be smaller attendances than for league matches. The players, though, accepted a reduced level of £100 for a win, £50 for a loss, and the show was on the road again. Keighley were in the 'Lancashire' group with relatively easy games, and won six of the eight matches to progress to a quarter-final at Workington, where two new young stars on loan from Leeds, the Gibbons twins, impressed in a 36-10 win.

The week before, more drama was unfolding as Cougars' chairman Carl Metcalfe sensationally quit because of alleged threats to his family and himself. He said he'd had enough - and, indeed, Metcalfe had been subjected to criticism and abuse from the start of his involvement with the club. Rumours of his possible departure had been circulating in March, but this was obviously the end. Metcalfe had become involved in the club without really knowing anything about rugby, and had promised the earth before he claimed that the horrendous debts the club had amassed made it impossible for him to deliver. It does seem, though, that he too, like everyone else who became involved, became seduced and captivated by the Cougar magic. Now, main sponsor Howard Carter became the acting chairman.

The Premiership semi-final was at home to Huddersfield, who had finished second in Division One. A respectable crowd of 3,480 on another lovely afternoon - summer rugby has a lot going for the spectators - saw an enthralling game. Huddersfield had to be favourites, but a young Keighley team played superbly in the first half and took an 8-0 lead. Dreams of a third successive appearance at Old Trafford were shattered, though, as Huddersfield got it together and finally won 18-8. They went on to beat Hull in the final, and before the end of the year had secured a place in Super League for 1998. Paris, that expensive and unnatural symbol of European expansion, dropped out, and Huddersfield were awarded their slot. Super League had begun on a heady night in March 1996 at the Charlety Stadium, home of Paris St Germain Football Club, with Sheffield the visitors - and the losers - and a crowd of 17,000. It was all an illusion, though. The French people in the crowd were only there because of a free ticket distribution, and their support for the Paris side waned alarmingly through the season. At first, the team actually had a respectable presence of French players in it, but by the 1997 season was stuffed full of Australian imports. Supporters from English clubs flocked to watch their team in Paris, but the French club had hardly any, perhaps no, following when they came to England. The truth was that few people in Paris could get worked up about an artificially-created side that had no heart and soul, and was located far from the traditional areas of support for rugby league in France. In 1997 the club proved an expensive white elephant as money was pumped in to try to shore it up - a privilege denied to struggling clubs in the north of England with a century of history. Huddersfield's admission to Super League was just one more irony for the Cougars. Two years earlier, Keighley had headed the First Division - above Hull and Huddersfield (not to mention London Broncos!) and been denied access. A year ago, they'd finished runners-up to Salford when only one promotion spot was available. Now, they were third, and had missed out again. Cougars had found themselves, once more, in the right place at the wrong time. But, of course, in 1997, there was a different equation: the team that would have served Keighley well in the top flight had gone. The semi-final marked the farewell game at Keighley for the club's other great Australian, Ian Gately, a particular favourite with the supporters. A special party was held the following Wednesday to honour him and say goodbye. But even the date of Ian's departure was imposed by financial considerations. Airline fares down under were set to rise for the Australian summer tourist season, so he and his family had to be on their way by the end of September. If Keighley had made it to the premiership final, Gately would not have played: his plane left Heathrow on the morning of the game.

Many people have criticised the number of overseas players in the English domestic game, but Ian Gately and Grant Doorey had immersed themselves in the Cougar ethos on both the playing and community side as much as anyone could have expected. They were a fine advert for Oz.

More departures took place in early October as Andy Eyres and Steve Hall were transferred to Rochdale, newly promoted from the second division, where they were joined by Keith Dixon after his brief sojourn at Dewsbury. Poor Steve Hall - his ambition had been to play at the top standard in the game, but Keighley's exclusion had thwarted that. Will he ever make it now? Commercial manager Norma Rankin also left, after 22 years at the club. She started as a part-time collector for the club lottery, and went on to be in charge of all the commercial operations in the club. Like many others, she cited her best memory as that evening in 1993 when Keighley beat Batley to lift the third division title.

Howard Carter, in the best traditions of Cougar news headlining, announced 'dynamic' plans for the next season, and John Kain said that a lot of promising players were interested in coming to Cougar Park. A Super League star was in the offing, if a local business could be persuaded to sponsor him. *Plus ça change...* Kain is a former Castleford player who had lots of coaching experience before he joined Cougars as Alliance team coach in 1994, but he faces a formidable task in trying to restore a semblance of recent glories.

Events elsewhere were conspiring to negate all those plans. The Rugby Football League Council - including the chief executive Maurice Lindsay, the RFL chairman Sir Rodney Walker, and the Featherstone Rovers chairman Steve Wagner - had decided it was time to recommend that those clubs which were in administration should be cut adrift on the grounds that they were a drain on the game in general. Accordingly, a special meeting of club chairmen was called for December 3rd to discuss the expulsion from the league of Keighley and another at-risk club, Workington Town. Prescot Panthers were also at risk, but because of their weak playing standard.

Peter O'Hara and Howard Carter moved to take steps to counter the threat, seeking assurances from the RFL that the club would not be ejected, and that money owing from the BSkyB TV deal would be paid without prejudice. Despite many communications, they found that no such assurance was forthcoming, so the club went to the High Court to get an injunction forbidding any discussion of the Keighley Cougars' situation at the meeting. A judge duly ruled on these counts, and the special meeting was informed of this fact as it was due to begun discussion on Keighley. Earlier, Workington had been reprieved - though ordered to play in the second division - after a rescue plan was approved, and Prescot's resignation from the league was accepted. A contingent of Keighley supporters travelled to Salford for the Council meeting in a protest reviving memories of 1995. Two days later, the RFL changed its mind and promised that Keighley would be able to take part in all competitions in 1998. Maurice Lindsay is adamant that he had never sought Keighley's expulsion - indeed, claims that it was the other First Division clubs that demanded that clubs in administration should receive no News Corporation money.

The only piece of the jigsaw now missing was the ending of administration, and this popped up in the shape of a Christmas present when Leeds financier and millionaire Hami Patel agreed to secure the club's future financially. This latest white knight is also a non-rugby person, but a close business colleague of Mike Smith, the same man who co-started Cougarism in 1991. Was this really the end of eighteen months of turmoil? Good news came thick and fast over the next few days. Lindsay said he welcomed the package and was pleased Keighley had got out of their difficulties. Simon Irving returned and was given a temporary contract as commercial manager.

Also back were two key players, Matt Foster and Rob Roberts, bought back from Leeds as part of the option under the deal of July 1997. Howard Carter became club chairman officially, with plans for 1998 that included a long-term coaching programme throughout the area, and a 'Cougar University' apprenticeship scheme. Simon Irving began making plans for business lunches. The sense of *deja vu* lay heavy on Cougar Park. But can it all happen again, or have we seen the best already? When you dream with the Cougars, anything is possible...... The bookmakers certainly thought so, and made Cougars favourites to win the First Division in 1998. This may have been unrealistically optimistic, and seemed based on the fact that the two sides who finished above Keighley in 1997 had gone into Super League.

The untimely death of catering manager Sue Loftus at the age of 40 early in 1998 underlined how much the club depended on a whole host of people who rarely, if ever, hit any headlines, but were absolutely vital in keeping things going. Sue had overseen the bar and players' meals for years, and was extremely popular at Cougar Park.

1998 - a journey of recovery

The new season began five weeks earlier than scheduled. The First and Second Divisions Association (FASDA), set up to look after the interests of clubs in those divisions after the creation of Super League Europe, decided that the originally scheduled 20-game season just wasn't long enough or financially viable. Accordingly, it was upped to 30-game length - each club would play every other one three times.

Keighley did not do much to inspire confidence with their first league match of the season, losing 16-41 at Swinton. Meanwhile, though, after a predictably comfortable 66-16 success against amateur side Saddleworth in their first game of the 1998 Challenge Cup, Cougars got what was probably the most exciting draw for the next round: a home game against Wigan, another full house, another great occasion at Cougar Park. Unfortunately, despite the fact that the match was made all-ticket, the anticipated big attendance didn't materialise, with just 4,700 present. Still, the fact that such a figure represents a disappointment shows how far the Cougar magic still obtained, and the attendance compared very favourably with other cup games that weekend. The much-hyped Leeds v. Castleford all Super League clash only attracted just over 7,000 spectators to Headingley. At Cougar Park, on a mid-February afternoon with a June temperature, not even diehard supporters could give Keighley any sort of chance. One confided before the game that he expected a 70-point defeat. He was pretty accurate. Wigan set off at a stunning pace and scored at the rate of a point a minute throughout the game. They paid Cougars the compliment of fielding a near full-strength team, and the stars ran through their repertoire. Home fans were unsure of how to take this one, but couldn't fail to appreciate the superb talents of Robinson, Paul, Farrell, Haughton, Radlinski, Connolly and company, making their first appearance at Cougar Park. It was

Gary Connolly tries to sidestep Chris Robinson as Wigan pile on the pressure (photo: Brian Lund)

February 1998 - Wigan supporters enjoy a rare chance to visit Cougar Park (photo: Brian Lund)

Keighley's biggest ever home defeat, but that wasn't the image that lingered after the game. Rather it was Jason Robinson and Simon Haughton, who stayed on the pitch for some fifteen minutes at the end, signing autographs for an insatiable stream of Keighley fans. The strains of Tina Turner's *'Simply the best'* came from the public address system. It was tempting to speculate on what might have happened had Wigan come to Cougar Park in February 1996... but that might be just too much dream-daring.

Cougarmania

The only surprise about the promotion of Keighley and its rugby league team in the early 1990s was that they didn't call the place Cougartown. The concept proved to be so successful that it enveloped whole swathes of community life, and the logo, emblazoned on replica shirts, sweaters, car stickers and posters, became a familiar and instantly recognisable sight. The club were not the first to adopt a catchy name, but they were the first to make it work. Sheffield had adopted the 'Eagles' name when they were formed in 1984, but never really got it into the city's consciousness. Huddersfield bizarrely became the 'Barracudas' during their final days at Fartown, but this caught on with nobody. Strangely, Castleford had already used the 'Cougar' name informally, but failed to register it. The 'Pirates' of Scarborough never developed any identity in the seaside town and folded after a couple of seasons. In Keighley, the Cougars became pioneers in the art of club and community bonding. Delegations from other clubs, including Bradford, came to see how it all worked. When Peter Deakin masterminded the transformation of Bradford from Northern to Bulls, it was Keighley's model he faithfully followed. After the start of Super League, an edict from RLHQ told all clubs to grab a nickname, but few have made it work. Some of the names chosen were ridiculous and unnecessary. Why did Wigan, the best rugby team in the world, need to adopt the appendage 'Warriors'? St. Helens decided they could manage quite well without one, and those teams with original names, such as Featherstone Rovers, felt they were better off sticking with tradition. In Keighley, Cougars very quickly *became* the tradition.

Cougarmania made its presence felt far beyond what might have been the normally expected catchment area, fuelled by features in national newspapers. It caught the attention of many Keighley folk who had strayed elsewhere, like Paul Aspinall in Nottinghamshire. Paul had been brought up on rugby league, becoming a programme seller at Lawkholme as a young lad. His father helped with administration at the club, and his older brother became a lifelong supporter, watching the team in bad and good times. Paul moved away at the age of 18, kept his love of the game alive following the Mansfield Marksmen during their brief and (mostly) inglorious history, but was drawn back by the lure of Cougarmania. He introduced his neighbours in the Notts village of Bingham to the game, and organised regular pilgrimages north, taking others with him. In such small ways was the gospel spread.

A dedication to the Cougars appeared in the tributes on the Oasis album *(What's the story) Morning glory?* (chief roadie Jason Rhodes is a Keighley fan!) and the players popped up on an episode of *Emmerdale*. Most of the first team appeared on the programme in 1995, along with Wigan (and, later, London Broncos) star Martin Offiah and Keighley chairman Mick O'Neill, who is a regular villager on the set.

Not everyone, of course, was instantly enamoured of the new style the club adopted when Cougarism began. Terry Hollindrake, perhaps the leading rugby icon in the town in 1991 for his exploits in the fifties and sixties, admits that he was initially unimpressed with the new name, the music and the general razz-ma-tazz. *"It was dreadful!"* he remembers. But once success arrived, he was converted, and, like most other people, became drawn in to the Cougar fantasy. Shirt designs for the Cougars gradually became more and more outrageous, but merely added to the sense of magic abroad at Cougar Park; in fact, by 1995, the gear actually made the players *look* like magicians.

The Cougar story is ongoing, and will hopefully merit a second edition of this book. But at the time of writing, the future is still uncertain. If the unravelling of the plot provides as much excitement as it has done for the past seven years, the town's rugby team may well keep Keighley in the headlines.

What went wrong?

When the world of Keighley Cougars seemed to fold in July 1997, people in Keighley felt betrayed. And not just the supporters, but townsfolk who, while they might never have gone to watch, still felt that the image of the town that the rugby league side had enabled had been shattered. Quite who they blamed was less easy to pinpoint. Certainly Maurice Lindsay, the perceived demon in 1995, was an easy target. Would things have been different if Cougars had stepped up to Super League in that first season? Phil Larder certainly believes that the club had a squad capable of finishing in the top half of the table. Mick O'Neill is convinced that *anything* was possible. The club lost potential revenue from sponsors, the certainty of increased support, and a huge handout from the BSkyB TV money.

It is certainly tempting to conclude that the world of the Cougars began to spiral out of control from that fateful Saturday when a Super League that didn't include Keighley was confirmed. Mike Smith certainly thinks so: the loss of sponsorship, the financial deadweight of full-time contracts, and the chance of increased gate revenue down the drain all added to the financial pressure on the club. Super League rejection placed a huge strain on the club, both financially and emotionally. But equally, the club made a conscious decision to go all out for the First Division Championship the following summer: there could be no turning back. If, at that stage, the club had decided to cut its losses, sell players, and sit back and settle for a cosy life in First Division mid-table, it would almost have been a denial of everything that had gone before: the euphoria of winning Division 3, the emotive response to the door to the top flight being closed, the Premiership glory, the hard, hard work that everyone - players, administrators, supporters, and the community itself had put in. The club was on a roll, and the momentum had to continue. This particular train could not stop. But, in the end, the 'all or nothing' strategy broke the bank. And when the players did go, next to nothing was realised for them, despite the fact that these were the club's chief assets. Even Pinkney and Wood went for a bargain fee for an international and a hugely influential team man.

Part of the problem arose from the fact that it would be the best part of the year from the decision to start Super League and the kick-off to the first summer season, and all that was in between was the short Centenary campaign and a Challenge Cup run. Full-time players had to be paid all the time, rugby or no rugby, and there is no doubt that by the time Keighley kicked off again in 1996, the financial strain was already immense. Money worries began to take their toll behind the scenes, and whereas the management style had been very positive and pro-active up to April 1995, the pressure began to tell from that point. Smith and O'Neill began to fall out - over serious issues like full-time contracts, but over trivial things as well, both conscious that they were at risk of letting down everyone who'd invested time, money and emotion in the Cougars.

Some supporters felt let down by successive directors, who had lived on a wing and a prayer, taken big risks, and thrown money at players in a desperate bid for success, projecting the club into tricky financial quicksands. Many also felt that they were not kept properly informed of what was really going on during the bad times.

"The club had terrific potential," believes Ian Gately, *"but injuries at vital times and the financial strictures helped to blow it."* As a result, much of the hard work has been devalued. Yet though the club now has a mostly new, inexperienced team, the ground improvements have given the club a springboard for the next move forward.

But whatever had happened, there was still lots to feel proud of. Keighley had started so much, been so innovative, provided an example to every other rugby club both on and off the field. In those four years of heady success, supporters had enjoyed moments of euphoria that can only be experienced by teams that challenge and upset the odds. Cougar fans had felt inspired, uplifted, emotionally fulfilled. Everyone who was part of the experience could feel privileged to have been there. It was summed up by a family at the Wigan game in February 1998: wife, husband and children, all enjoying the atmosphere, the rugby, the experience. They had been cougarised back in 1993, and had loved it. *"We've been all over watching Cougars, including Wembley and Old Trafford, and had a fantastic time."* Like thousands of other families, the Cougars had impacted on their lives in a wholly positive way.

Mike Smith and Mick O'Neill, the directors who'd provided the vision and the impetus to make it possible, had created something that had always seemed impossible at Keighley. They had, in Smith's words, *"dared to dream."*

Super League - and a month that stunned the Cougars

The exclusion of Keighley from the proposed Super League was seen in the town as a truly bizarre decision, but no dafter than the composition of this new league as a whole. The initially favoured teams, including a selection of proposed mergers, appear to have been the product of something akin to the fantasy rugby that youngsters used to invent and which now appears in reputable newspapers and magazines as a fun game. None of the mergers materialised, because of hostility from clubs and supporters themselves. Even the two Hull outfits failed to make progress on negotiations, each preparing to take its chance of getting into Super League at some future date on its own merits. The second French club never happened, though the Paris team was launched successfully when Super League began in March 1996. Wales, too, didn't get a team. London Broncos were considered crucial to the expansion that it was hoped would now be set in motion, but they had to be leapfrogged above three other second division sides to get them there. In the end, the twelve-team league contained ten familiar names. Keighley were not the only club that could feel hard done to - Widnes, Salford, Wakefield, Featherstone and Batley (the latter Division 2 runners-up at the end of season 1994-95) could all justifiably feel aggrieved - but Keighley's case was strong. Their exclusion flew in the face of natural sporting justice, for all league systems depend for their appeal on a sensible system of promotion and relegation. Clubs and supporters need the promise of top league status if they are successful in a lower one. Football and rugby union do not operate a cosy protective system for their top teams, and nor do they exclude clubs on spurious grounds. Wimbledon's rise to Premier League status was a rags to riches story to inspire every other lowly team, and the fact they haven't got a ground of their own hasn't got them kicked out of football's top competition. Barnsley may not be able to survive in football's top flight, but they have earned the right to be there, and their players and supporters are entitled to savour the season. Ground capacity rules can be a red herring, too. No-one suggests that Bath shouldn't be in rugby union's division one just because their ground holds no more spectators than Keighley's. All the excuses for denying Keighley a Super League place cannot hide the fact that a serious natural injustice was perpetrated. The club would have brought a passion and excitement to Super League that was not always evident elsewhere.

One easy solution to the problem would have been to extend the inaugural league to 14 clubs - or even 16 - which would have accommodated two or four other sides who merited a place. But that, of course, would have meant spreading the Murdoch money a touch more thinly, and the favoured clubs would have got a smaller share each. In view of the fact that after a couple of seasons, every club was complaining about two few home games and too short a playing season, it would have been far more sensible to have had two divisions of 16 rather than split the professional teams into three leagues. The whole plan was put together so quickly that it is tempting to think that the implications of what was happening had not been seriously considered.

Three and a half years on from the Murdoch offer, it is plain that the game as a whole is no better off, and that too much of the money so far spent has gone on players' wages and transfer fees, as clubs continue to pursue the Holy Grail of Super League or bust. "The Murdoch money," wrote Simon Kelner in his excellent RL history 'To Jerusalem and back,' "must not be allowed simply to slip into the pockets of players, or be used to pay the salaries of a new breed of chief executives and marketing managers, or be frittered away on half-baked promotional initiatives, or be allowed to prop up Paris or London if they appear to be failing. It must be put towards the refurbishment of stadiums, development of the game at junior levels, and to nourish clubs where there is proven potential, even if they are outside the Super League." Some hope! All Kelner's fears have taken place, with the exception of London Broncos who, although cosseted by a generous overseas player allowance, have at least been positive and imaginative in their ideas and performances, and have now secured the backing of Britain's most charismatic businessman, Richard Branson. Otherwise, the worst has happened, and today more clubs are on the breadline than in 1994. Two, Workington and Oldham, who received respectively one and two years of BSkyB handouts, contrived to go bankrupt, though both, like Keighley, have come through their own traumas: Oldham actually collapsed and were pronounced dead, but then rose Phoenix-like under a new board, and were re-admitted to the 2nd Division. Public perception of, and interest in, rugby league throughout Britain is probably lower after two seasons of Super League than it was before Murdoch arrived. The game is virtually confined to a minority channel, so its exposure has been reduced, not heightened. Surely it would have been more sensible to have renegotiated the super RL product with the BBC, which is now crying out for an entertaining sport to show on its screens? Perhaps the News Corporation offer should have been used as a lever?

Super League as a concept was an excellent idea, and summer rugby has been a reasonable success, but the timetable of the implementation of the plan meant that some clubs were caught awkwardly on the shifting sands. Four days in April 1994 might just have been a touch too hasty, a decision too rushed, and a headlong race to an uncertain future. That future continues to look hazy. At the time of writing, the recently-formed Association of First and Second Division Clubs (FASDA) is planning its own sponsorship and possibly contemplating a return to winter rugby, and the Super League clubs, now with their separate organisation, will negotiate any future News Corporation deal on their own. Maurice Lindsay is now chief executive of Super League Europe, and the Rugby League itself has a new head, Neil Tunnicliffe. It may well be that within a short space of time, the Super League will have combined with the top Rugby Union clubs under communal sponsorship, playing a hybrid game - and the Featherstones, Swintons and Keighleys will be guardians of the traditional game, playing again in a winter season.

KEIGHLEY R.L.F.C.   **RESULTS & SCORERS**   **SEASON 1992-93**

Date	Opponents	H/A	Comp	Result	Tries	Goals	Drop Goals
Aug-30	Workington T	H	D3	W18-2	Hinchliffe, Eyres	Wasyliw (5)	
Sep-06	Hunslet	A	D3	L12-28	Hinchliffe, Kerr	Wasyliw (2)	
Sep-13	Nottingham C	H	YC	W30-4	Walker, Race, Ramshaw, Wood	Wasyliw (7)	
Sep-20	Barrow	H	D3	W40-10	Appleby (2), Walker (2), Race, Wasyliw	Wasyliw (8)	
Sep-23	Wakefield T	A	YC	L16-22	Appleby, Ramshaw, Eyres	Wasyliw (2)	
Sep-27	Dewsbury	A	D3	L13-24	Grima	Wasyliw (4)	Wood
Oct-04	Chorley B	A	D3	W54-12	Wasyliw (2), Dixon (2), Wood (2), Appleby, Hinchliffe, Ball	Wasyliw (9)	
Oct-22	Whitehaven	A	D3	W18-8	Race, Wood, Wasyliw	Wasyliw (3)	
Nov-01	Nottingham C	H	D3	W86-0	Wood (3), Eyres (2), Moses (2), Appleby (2), Farrell, Grima, Ball, Brooke-Cowden, Wasyliw	Wasyliw (15)	
Nov-08	Leigh	A	RT	L24-32	Wasyliw (2), Appleby (2)	Wasyliw (4)	
Nov-22	Highfield	H	D3	W44-10	Gately (2), Appleby (2), Grima, Hiley, Moses, Wasyliw	Wasyliw (6)	
Nov-29	Ryedale-York	A	D3	W16-14	Wasyliw, Moses	Wasyliw (4)	
Dec-13	Whitehaven	H	D3	L8-21	A.Stephenson	Wasyliw (2)	
Dec-20	Nottingham C	A	D3	W42-2	Ramshaw (2), Appleby (2), Hall, Reeves	Wasyliw (9)	
Jan-10	Workington T	A	D3	W21-0	Farrell, Wood, Hall, Wasyliw	Wasyliw (2)	Ramshaw
Jan-13	Doncaster	H	D3	W31-10	Wasyliw (2), Farrell, Moses, Wood, Ramshaw	Wasyliw (3)	Dixon
Jan-20	Blackpool G	H	D3	W36-4	Dixon (2), Wood (2), Appleby, Hall, Wasyliw	Wasyliw (4)	
Jan-31	Highfield	H	RLC	W86-0	Appleby (3), Dixon (2), Milner (2), Ramshaw (2), Brooke-Cowden, Race, Farrell, Gately, Wasyliw, Wood	Wasyliw (13)	
Feb-07	Ryedale-York	H	D3	W22-15	Ball, Race, Wood	Wasyliw (5)	
Feb-14	Hull K.R.	A	RLC	L28-30	Wasyliw (2), Moses, Wood	Wasyliw (6)	
Feb-21	Chorley B	H	D3	W78-6	Milner (4), Dixon (3), Ramshaw (2), Wasyliw (2), Eyres, Grima, Hiley, A.Stephenson	Wasyliw (9)	
Feb-28	Barrow	A	D3	W42-20	Eyres (2), Wasyliw (2), Dixon, Farrell, Wood	Wasyliw (7)	
Mar-07	Blackpool G	A	D3	W82-8	Wood (4), Eyres (2), A.Stephenson (2), Hiley, McAlister, Milner, Ramshaw, Smith, Wasyliw	Wasyliw (13)	
Mar-14	Dewsbury	H	D3	W33-24	Eyres, Grima, Hiley, Wood, Ramshaw	Wasyliw (6)	Dixon
Mar-16	Highfield	A	D3	W80-8	Wasyliw (3), Milner (2), Farrell, A.Stephenson (2), Wood (2), Eyres, Gately	Wasyliw (10)	
Mar-28	Hunslet	H	D3	W49-8	Milner (2), Wasyliw (2), Wood (2), Eyres, Walker	Wasyliw (8)	Eyres
Apr-04	Doncaster	A	D3	W32-30	Dixon, Farrell, Gately, Milner, Race, Wood	Wasyliw (4)	
Apr-09	Batley	H	D3	W34-10	A.Stephenson (2), Eyres, Farrell, Gately, Hall	Wasyliw (5)	
Apr-12	Batley	A	D3	W26-14	McAlister (2), Race (2), Wasyliw	Wasyliw (3)	
Apr-18	Hunslet	H	DP	W34-6	Wood (2), Brooke-Cowden, Race, McAlister, Wasyliw	Wasyliw (5)	
Apr-25	Rochdale H	A	DP	L18-26	Grima, Wasyliw	Wasyliw (4)	Dixon, Ramshaw

The Third Division Championship season, with only 3 games lost out of 24.

Joe Grima and the side after winning the Third Division Championship in 1992-93 (photo: Peter Stell)

Peter Roe, who coached the team to the title in 1992-93 (photo: Peter Stell)

Chris Robinson sends out a pass during the Premiership semi-final game against Huddersfield in September 1997 (photo: Brian Lund)

Below: Mick O'Neill and Mike Smith show off the Second Division Championship Trophy

Freddy Cougar

KEIGHLEY R.L.F.C.   **RESULTS & SCORERS**   **SEASON 1994-95**

Date	Opponents	H/A	Comp	Result	Tries	Goals	Drop Goals
Aug-21	Whitehaven	H	D2	W38-8	Pinkney (3), Walker (2), Appleby, Eyres	Walker (4), Wood	
Aug-28	Rochdale H	A	D2	W30-16	Pinkney (2), Stoop, Creasser, Walker, Stephenson	Creasser (3)	
Sep-04	Ryedale-York	H	D2	D18-18	Hill (2), Dixon, Stoop	Creasser	
Sep-11	London B	A	D2	W30-10	Wood (2), Irving, Ramshaw, Stoop	Irving (5)	
Sep-18	Dewsbury	H	D2	W46-8	Wood (2), Eyres, Gately, Irving, Pinkney, Stoop	Irving (9)	
Sep-25	Bramley	A	D2	W18-2	Eyres, Kenyon, Stoop	Irving (3)	
Oct-02	Barrow	A	D2	W24-10	Cochrane, Dixon, Hall	Irving (6)	
Oct-09	Batley	H	D2	L22-26	Eyres, Irving, Pinkney	Irving (5)	
Oct-16	Hunslet	H	D2	W66-10	Pinkney (5), Stoop (2), Dixon, Eyres, Fleary, Irving, Kenyon, Wood	Irving (7)	
Oct-30	Carlisle	H	D2	W46-14	Pinkney (4), Eyres, Fleary, Hill, Irving, Walker	Irving (5)	
Nov-06	Whitehaven	A	D2	W38-8	Irving (2), Pinkney (2), Doorey, Eyres	Irving (7)	
Nov-13	Rochdale H	H	D2	W28-13	Dixon, Irving, Pinkney, Walker	Irving (6)	
Nov-27	Chorley	H	RT	W56-0	Pinkney (3), Walker (3), Doorey, Hall, Gibson, Larder, Ramshaw, Wood	Walker (4)	
Dec-04	Bramley	H	RT	W28-4	Hall (2), Pinkney (2), Robinson, Stoop	Irving (2)	
Dec-11	Ryedale-York	A	D2	W52-12	Dixon (3), Ramshaw (2), Gately, Hill, Irving, Pinkney, Wood	Irving (6)	
Dec-18	Sheffield E	H	RT	W26-10	Cochrane, Dixon, Robinson, Stoop	Irving (5)	
Dec-26	Hull K.R.	H	D2	W24-12	Eyres, Pinkney, Robinson, Stephenson	Irving (4)	
Dec-31	Huddersfield	A	D2	W15-10	Irving, Ramshaw	Irving (3)	Ramshaw
Jan-08	Warrington	H	RT	L18-20	Eyres, Pinkney, Stoop	Irving (3)	
Jan-11	London B	H	D2	L14-25	Dixon (2)	Irving (3)	
Jan-15	Swinton	A	D2	W48-6	Wood (2), Cochrane, Eyres, Irving, Pinkney, P.Stephenson, Stoop	Irving (8)	
Jan-24	Chorley	H	RLC	W68-0	Dixon (2), Larder (2), Irving (2), Appleby, Berry, Delaney, Eyres, Hill, Kenyon, Pinkney, Ramshaw	Irving (6)	
Feb-01	Leigh	H	D2	W38-6	Eyres (2), Dixon, Doorey, Pinkney, Stoop, Wood	Irving (5)	
Feb-05	Bramley	H	D2	W24-8	Eyres (3), Pinkney, Stoop	Irving (2)	
Feb-12	Dewsbury	H	RLC	W24-12	Pinkney (2), Cochrane, Irving, Robinson	Irving (2)	
Feb-19	Barrow	H	D2	W28-6	Appleby, Dixon, Doorey, Pinkney, Wray	Dixon (4)	
Feb-26	Huddersfield	H	RLC	L0-30			
Mar-06	Batley	A	D2	L6-8	Pinkney	Irving	
Mar-12	Highfield	H	D2	W68-0	Eyres (3), Irving (3), Appleby (2), Dixon (2), Doorey, Gately	Irving (9), Dixon	
Mar-19	Hunslet	A	D2	W33-18	Gately (2), Appleby, Fleary, Wood	Irving (6)	Ramshaw
Mar-22	Dewsbury	A	D2	L2-20		Irving	
Mar-26	Carlisle	A	D2	L2-12		Irving	
Apr-02	Leigh	A	D2	W34-13	Kenyon (2), Pinkney (2), Eyres, Ramshaw	Wood (5)	
Apr-09	Swinton	H	D2	W42-6	Kenyon (3), Wood (3), Race, Robinson	Wood (5)	
Apr-14	Hull K.R.	A	D2	W14-6	Ramshaw, Wood	Wood (3)	
Apr-17	Huddersfield	H	D2	D22-22	Cochrane, Eyres, Irving, Pinkney	Irving (2), Wood	
Apr-23	Highfield	A*	D2	W104-4	Pinkney (5), Eyres (3), Ramshaw (3), Wood (2), Cochrane, Dixon, Hill, Irving, Kenyon, Powell, Robinson	Irving (12)	
May-07	Hull K.R.	H	SDP	W42-16	Dixon (2), Irving (2), Powell (2), Hill	Irving (7)	
May-14	London B	H	SDP	W38-4	Wood (2), Irving, Pinkney, Robinson, Stoop	Irving (7)	
May-21	Huddersfield	N*	SDP	W26-6	Eyres, Pinkney, Powell, Wood	Irving (4)	Ramshaw (2)

A* - match played at Spotland, Rochdale
N* - Premiership Final played at Old Trafford, Manchester

The best-ever? The Second Division Championship and the Premiership, and a good run in the Regal Trophy.

Keighley 'B.C.' - The way it used to be

Mike Smith talked of a 'complete culture change' when the Cougars were launched, but it must not be forgotten that the club actually had 115 years of history in various guises, and that it had been part of the Northern Union/ Rugby League for 91 years. Anything that happened prior to 1991 is now referred to as 'B.C.' (Before Cougars) by current programme editor Mike Ford, and the remainder of this book provides a potted history of what went before. It is a series of snapshots, not an attempt at a definitive history, to give a flavour of those years.

A promising start

Though the club was formed to play rugby in October 1876, it was not until 1900 that Keighley followed the example of those clubs which had broken away from the Rugby Football Union in 1895 to form the 'Northern Union.' The club's entry to this new world was at first highly promising. In the Yorkshire section of what was effectively a second team competition for the first two seasons, the team finished second and third, and then won a new second division in 1902-3, with only five defeats in 34 games. Among the players that appeared that season were Harry Myers, the captain, Harry Holden, Bob Walker, Alf and Ned Pearson, B. Sharpe, Chris Hardacre, Ike Jagger, Charlie Caine, J.W. Fearnley, J. Hall, S. Liddemore, Hartley Tempest, J. Kilbey, J. Royston, Ned Dawson, T. Holmes, Arthur Slater, Charlie Saunders, and H. Dixon. They came straight back at the end of the following season, and then finished fourth in Division 2. From 1905, clubs played in one single league until a two-division format was tried again in 1962, an experiment that lasted just two seasons. In the first five years of that single competition, Keighley finished in the top five on three occasions, figuring in the top four play-offs in 1907, and reaching the semi-final of the Northern Union Challenge Cup in 1906, losing 3-6 to Salford after claiming the scalps of Castleford, Egremont, Hull and Featherstone Rovers. The semi-final nearly had to be surrendered, though: Keighley players were hugely dissatisfied on the eve of the game with the payment terms offered, and threatened to pull out. The following season saw a sporting tragedy. Harry Myers, Keighley's inspiration for ten years, was badly injured during a game at Dewsbury in November, and died later in hospital.

The New Zealand touring team played at Lawkholme in November 1907, and the Australians made their first visit in January 1909.

St. Helens' visit for a third round cup game in 1915 proved a memorable game, in fact the last one at Lawkholme for four and a half years. With the scores level at 0-0 at full-time, extra time was played under wartime rules. Charlie Taylor dropped a goal for Keighley, but with home fans high on the prospect of a semi-final appearance, Trenwith scored a controversial try for Saints to win them the match. A demonstration against Bradford referee Bob Robinson after the game by a section of the Keighley crowd led to the ground being suspended for the rest of the season - effectively just one match, played at Birch Lane, Bradford.

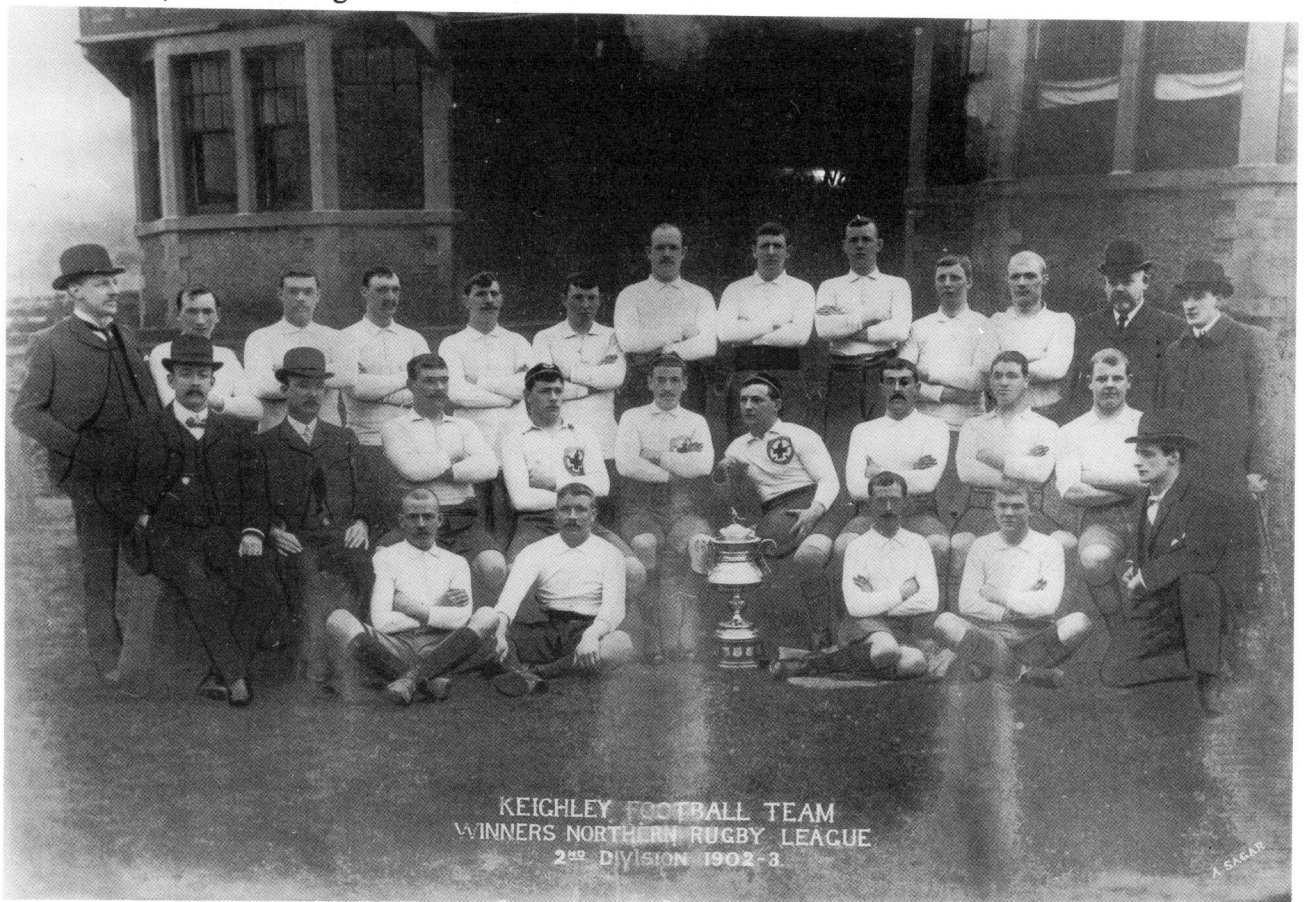

The team and backroom boys that won the 2nd Division Championship in 1902-3 season. Back: L. Jackson (groundsman), H. Dixon, E. Pearson, C. Hardacre, C. Saunders, J. Collins, H. Holden, T. Holmes, F. Royston, J. Bradley, J. Hall, Mr Elgie (county and league representative), Cpt C.P. Cass (President). Middle: G.B. Whitaker (vice-president), L. Greetham (secretary), J.W. Fearsley, H. Tempest, I. Jugger, H. Myers, R. Walker, A. Slater, E. Dawson. Front: C. Kilbey, S. Liddemore, A. Pickering, ?, H. Hoyle (trainer)

KEIGHLEY R.L.F.C.　　　　**RESULTS & SCORERS**　　　　　　　　　　**SEASON 1902-03**

Date	Opponents	H/A	Comp	Result	Tries	Goals
Sep-06	York	A	D2	D3-3	Myers	
Sep-13	Barrow	H	D2	W12-5	Myers, Jagger	E.Pearson (2), Myers
Sep-20	Millom	H	D2	W7-0	Fearnley	Pearson, Myers
Sep-27	Wakefield T	A	D2	W12-10	A.Pearson, Holmes	Walker (2), E.Pearson
Oct-04	Morecambe	H	D2	W16-0	A.Pearson, Myers, Pickering, Hall	Myers, E.Pearson
Oct-11	Dewsbury	A	D2	W6-0	Pickering, T.Holmes	
Oct-18	Brighouse	H	O	D0-0		
Oct-25	Bramley	A	D2	L3-6	Holden	
Nov-01	Rochdale H	H	D2	W11-8	Pickering, A.Pearson, Hardacre	Myers
Nov-08	Castleford	H	D2	W10-3	Myers, A.Pearson	Myers (2)
Nov-15	Normanton	H	D2	D0-0		
Nov-22	Manningham	H	D2	W15-0	A.Pearson, Tempest, Kilbey	E.Pearson (3)
Nov-29	Stockport	H	D2	W19-0	T.Holmes(2), Myers, Collins, Hardacre	E.Pearson, Myers
Dec-06	Lancaster	A	D2	W10-0	Hardacre, Myers	E.Perason, Walker
Dec-13	Leeds	H	D2	W13-2	Jagger, Saunders, Caine	E.Pearson (2)
Dec-20	Holbeck	A	D2	L0-8		
Dec-25	South Shields	H	D2	W3-0	Tempest	
Dec-26	Bramley	H	D2	W9-0	Myers	E.Pearson (2), Myers
Dec-27	Birkenhead	H	D2	W8-0	Royston, Myers	E.Pearson
Jan-03	York	H	D2	W7-0	A.Pearson	E.Pearson (2)
Jan-10	Barrow	A	D2	W5-0	Saunders	E.Pearson
Jan-24	Wakefield T	H	D2	W16-2	A.Pearson (2), Myers, Saunders	E.Pearson (2)
Jan-31	Morecambe	A	D2	W8-6		E.Pearson (2), A.Pearson, B.Sharpe
Feb-02	Millom	A	D2	W2-0		Walker
Feb-07	Dewsbury	H	D2	W8-0	Jagger, Holden	Myers
Feb-14	Heckmondwike	H	YC	W37-0	Myers (3), Hardacre (2), Jagger, A.Pearson (2), E.Pearson	Myers (3), Caine (2)
Feb-24	Manningham	H	YC	W12-0	Hardacre (2)	Myers (2), Hardacre
Feb-28	Rochdale H	A	D2	W5-0	Hardacre	Myers
Mar-07	York	H	YC	D2-2		Myers
Mar-11	York	A	YC	L9-12	A.Pearson	Myers (3)
Mar-14	Normanton	A	D2	L11-15	A.Pearson (2), Myers	Myers
Mar-21	Manningham	A	D2	W10-0	Hardacre, Saunders	Myers, Hardacre
Mar-28	Stockport	A	D2	W13-0	Hardacre (2), Myers	Myers (2)
Apr-04	Lancaster	H	D2	W2-0		Sharpe
Apr-06	Castleford	A	D2	W7-0	Jagger	Myers (2)
Apr-11	Leeds	A	D2	L0-19		
Apr-13	South Shields	A	D2	W5-2	Jagger	E.Pearson
Apr-14	Bradford	A	F	L14-23	Jagger, Caine	Walker (3), Caine
Apr-18	Holbeck	H	D2	W12-0	A.Pearson (2)	Myers (2), Caine
Apr-25	Birkenhead	A	D2	L2-3		Myers

This is the first of six season summaries that are included in this book. It features results from 1902-03, when Keighley won promotion after heading Division 2. There are some unfamiliar names among the opponents, including South Shields, Lancaster and Morecambe.

Photo by Scott & Co   KEIGHLEY R.F.C.   Published by J. Booth, Leeds.
W T Drummond, J Narey, E Dawson, T Hopkinson, J Pickles, T Hardwick, A Wilkinson
J Winterburn, A Bateson, H Tempest, R Walker, (Capt.) J Jagger, H Holden, W Hunt, L Greetham, (Sec.)
B Craven,   S Stacey,   W Madley

The 1905-6 Keighley team on a postcard published by Booth of Leeds. Among the players are Ike Jagger and Sam Stacey, both of whom scored five tries in a game. Stacey and Tempest are profiled in this book.

The Lawkholme Lane ground c. 1910. The barn seen in this picture was demolished in April 1933

JACK S. FEATHER, PRINTER.   KEIGHLEY N.U.F.C. SEASON 1920-21.   PHOTO—BRUCE JOHNSTONE

A picture postcard of the 1920-21 squad

William Yiend does not really belong to Keighley's Rugby League history, for he left Keighley long before they joined the Northern Union in 1900. He does, though, deserve a mention in Keighley's history because he was captain of the side when Keighley played their first match on the current ground at Lawkholme Lane in 1885 - indeed it was he who kicked off in that first match. Yiend left Keighley to go to Hartlepool Rovers, where he gained international honours, playing for England on four occasions. Subsequent to playing rugby, Yiend took to refereeing and took at least one county match between Yorkshire and Cumberland on 4th March 1899, which was played at Lawkholme Lane and which included two Keighley players, J.Glew and A.W.Robinson, in the Yorkshire team.

Richard Kendall was one of the few - maybe the only - Keighley player to participate in the game of Rugby League as a player, coach, committee man, touch judge and referee. He joined Keighley in 1922 from Askam and, before signing for the club, played in an "A" team game witnessed by 2,000 spectators. That was the level of interest shown in his first appearance in a Keighley shirt when he played as "A.N.Other" alongside another trialist "A.Goodman" who was in reality Gilbert Rorison, another player from Cumbria to join the ranks of the Lawkholmers. That was 4th November 1922, and the following week he made his debut in the senior team against Featherstone Rovers. A winger who was also a useful goal kicker, in all he played 231 times for the club, scoring 55 tries and 185 goals, and in the 1929/30 season he became the first player for 20 years to score more than 100 points for the club in a season. His career flourished despite a series of injuries which would have brought any other player to an early retirement. Kendall broke his left collar bone twice, his right collar bone once, fractured his left fore-arm, broke bones in his right hand and wrist and sustained a variety of finger injuries. In September 1932 he was appointed assistant trainer and coach to the Keighley team before taking up flag waving and whistle blowing, first as a touch judge, then as a referee. In October 1934, he was a touch judge in the Yorkshire Cup Final between Leeds and Wakefield Trinity and in the 1945/46 season he made his debut as a first class referee, refereeing, among others, the cup tie between St. Helens and Castleford in February 1946. He also officiated as touch judge in the 1946 Cup Final between Wakefield Trinity and Wigan at Wembley and refereed several international matches.

Sam Stacey was one of those two players who, in the early years of this century, set a Keighley club record which was not equalled for 87 years, at least not in competitive rugby, and was not beaten for a further two years. It was equalled in a friendly match when, in 1951, Bill Ivill scored five times against Ystradgynlais. Sam Stacey was a wing threequarter and a prolific try scorer when scoring tries was not as easy or as frequent as today. Another winger, Ike Jagger, had scored five tries in the match against Castleford on 13th January 1906 and Stacey, who also scored two tries in that match, equalled the mark with five in the match against Liverpool City just over a year later on 9th March 1907. Stacey made his debut for Keighley on 17th October 1903 and played 283 times for Keighley before his career ended on 28th August 1920. Stacey scored 161 tries for the club in all, and it is incredible that Stacey's statistics were achieved with a period of inactivity lasting four seasons when play was suspended for the duration of the Great War. It is interesting to note that in the 1919/20 season, Stacey was the team's top try scorer with four tries, the team scoring only 25 tries in the whole season. In competitive matches, Stacey notched 155 tries in his career, a record which still stands in 1997. Stacey gained county honours when he represented Yorkshire on seven occasions.

David McGoun shares the Keighley club record for appearances in a career with Hartley Tempest at 372, in McGoun's case set between 1925 and 1938. His career at Keighley included three matches against touring sides, New Zealand in 1926 and Australia in 1929 and 1933, but he was unlucky to miss out on Keighley's one Challenge Cup Final appearance in 1937, which happened to be his benefit year. It was noted at the time that he was the only native of Keighley to be playing regularly that season! Yes, he played 24 times that season, but not at Wembley. McGoun was a prop forward, and a hard working one at that, so he did not have the scoring opportunities of some of his colleagues. Nevertheless he did manage nine tries and three goals in his Keighley career. McGoun may not have hit the headlines as far as his play was concerned, but his service to the team and club were valuable and it was certainly appreciated by the local supporters, to whom he was one of the most popular players.

A native of Haworth, ***Hartley Tempest*** was there almost at the beginning of Keighley's involvement with Rugby League, for he joined the club in October 1902 and went on to make 372 appearances for the club, a club record he shares with David McGoun, before the First World War brought his playing days to an end. Tempest was capped by Yorkshire on 14th April 1903 when he played alongside Harry Myers against Durham & Northumberland at South Shields. For them both it was their only appearance for the county as rugby league players. For Keighley, Tempest was a versatile forward who could and did play in almost every position in the pack during his career. It was a career which saw him play alongside some of Keighley's greats including Bob Walker, Sam Stacey, Ike Jagger, Charlie Taylor and, of course, the legendary Harry Myers.

Harry Myers was a half-back of great skill, and his abilities and influence had a great bearing on the progress made by the club at the turn of the century. Before Keighley joined the Northern Union, Myers was involved as Keighley's captain as the team won the Yorkshire Second Competition in 1897 and then the First Competition in the 1899/1900 season, having finished 2nd the year before. His goal kicking had been just as important as his ball handling and forays from the base of the scrum, and he captained the team for 10 of his 11 years at Lawkholme. It is a measure of Myers' skill that he is the only Keighley player to have played for England at Rugby Union, an achievement which was gained in February 1898 when he played against Ireland at Twickenham. Myers was also one of a handful of Keighley players to represent Yorkshire, gaining 13 caps before Keighley turned to Rugby League. It was Myers who captained the side when the team won the 2nd Division Championship in 1902/3 and reached the Challenge Cup Semi-Finals in 1905/6. He made the ultimate sacrifice for the Keighley club, though, when he died in December 1906 as a result of injuries sustained a month earlier in a match against Dewsbury at Crown Flatt. His influence, however, lived on as Keighley went on to qualify for the Championship play-off at the end of the season after finishing in 4th position in the league.

Action from the game between Keighley and the Australians on 1st October 1929

KEIGHLEY R.L.F.C.   RESULTS & SCORERS   SEASON 1925-26

Date	Opponents	H/A	Comp	Result	Tries	Goals
Aug-29	Hunslet	H	RL	W9-3	Perkins	Mitchinson, Pearson, Holmes
Sep-05	Huddersfield	A	RL	L2-26		Kendall
Sep-12	Bramley	H	RL	W33-3	Perkins (2), Kendall, Thompson, Craven (2), Holmes	Kendall (6)
Sep-16	Wakefield T	A	RL	L3-16	Perkins	
Sep-19	Hull K.R.	A	RL	L3-13	Perkins	
Sep-22	Wakefield T	H	RL	W16-4	Craven (2), Gill, Donovan	Kendall, Mitchinson
Oct-03	Featherstone	H	RL	W15-5	Holmes (2), Thompson	Kendall, Pearson (2)
Oct-10	Featherstone	H	YC	L4-18		Pearson (2)
Oct-17	Dewsbury	A	RL	L5-11	Kendall	Pearson
Oct-24	Rochdale H	A	RL	L5-26	Watson	Pearson
Oct-31	Halifax	H	RL	W8-0	Spedding, Kendall	Pearson
Nov-07	Hull	A	RL	L7-18	Pearson	Pearson (2)
Dec-05	Halifax	A	RL	L3-17	Kendall	
Dec-12	Barrow	A	RL	L3-11	Perkins	
Dec-19	Leeds	H	RL	L2-16		Pearson
Dec-25	Bradford N	H	RL	W11-5	Perkins, Holmes, Spavin	Pearson
Dec-26	York	A	RL	L3-25	Donovan	
Dec-28	York	H	RL	L3-5	Holmes	
Jan-02	Batley	A	RL	W5-4	Spavin	Pearson
Jan-09	Rochdale H	H	RL	L3-10	Thornton	
Jan-16	Hull	H	RL	D15-15	Donovan (2), Kendall	Kendall (3)
Jan-23	Featherstone	A	RL	L8-20	Kendall, Spavin	L.Foster
Jan-30	Barrow	H	RL	L9-22	Spavin, Thorpe, Kendall	
Feb-06	Hunslet	A	RL	L5-46	Holmes	Langhorn
Feb-13	Bradford N	A	RLC	D2-2		Kendall
Feb-17	Bradford N	A	RLC	D5-5	Thorpe	Kendall
Feb-20	Hull K.R.	H	RL	L9-10	Williams	Kendall (3)
Feb-22	Bradford N	A	RLC	L4-9		Thornton, Kendall
Feb-27	Salford	A	RL	L2-11		Kendall
Mar-06	Huddersfield	H	RL	L6-22	Langhorn, Craven	
Mar-13	Batley	H	RL	L5-7	Donovan	Langhorn
Mar-16	Warrington	H	RL	W26-7	Kendall (2), Trusler, Pearson, Watson, Thorpe	Kendall (3), Pearson
Mar-20	Bramley	A	RL	W2-0		Langhorn
Mar-27	St.Helens	A	RL	L10-34	Donovan, Kendall	Pearson (2)
Apr-02	Dewsbury	H	RL	L8-11	Kendall, Craven	Kendall
Apr-03	Leeds	A	RL	L24-60	Williams (2), Kendall, Thorpe, Holmes, Todd	Pearson (2), Kendall
Apr-05	Bradford N	A	RL	L10-36	Gill, Williams	Kendall (2)
Apr-06	St.Helens	H	RL	L2-12		Spavin
Apr-10	Salford	H	RL	L5-6	Pearson	Kendall
Apr-14	Warrington	A	RL	L5-40	Williams	Pearson

1925-26 was typical of Keighley's poor performances in the fifteen years after the First World War. With only 9 wins in 36 games, the club finished next to bottom of a single league. The Challenge Cup provided three tense games against local rivals Bradford Northern.

The desperate twenties

The period from the end of the First World War to the early thirties was a depressing one for the club. In thirteen seasons, Keighley finished in the bottom four on seven occasions, and only once inside the top twenty in a single league that fluctuated between 25 and 29 clubs.

Happily, though, the supporters' club was formed at this time. It was decided to start it at a special general meeting of the rugby club in the Devonshire Hotel on 10th February 1921. The motivation was, as ever, a financial crisis: the club was £555 in debt to the bank and needed baling out. The new supporters' club couldn't wave a magic wand, but it did hand over £400 during its first three seasons, and established a boys' team, which produced nine players who signed for the senior team. Part of the money donated was used to buy players. The rugby club severed its connection with the supporters' club in 1929 when it became a limited company, but the supporters' club continued to function, and over the years was to prove vital for the continued existence of the parent club.

The adventurous thirties

After a bleak decade, the pre-war period at least gave some pride back to the town and its rugby team. Season 1931-2 was a poor one, and directors Booth and Harrison decided some fresh initiatives were needed. Some attractive signings were the answer, so in came Joe Sherburn from Halifax, Tommy Davies from Wakefield, and the biggest capture of all - New Zealander Ted Spillane from Wigan. His first game for the club, against Huddersfield at Lawkholme, was an unexpected 19-0 victory for the home side against a team that had got used to recording big wins against Keighley. Spillane, of course, scored the try of the match, and his name provided the main topic of conversation in the town for weeks. Attendances shot up from 2,000 to over 5,000 as more major signings were announced: Hal Jones and George Dixon came from Wigan, and Jimmy Gill from Leeds. The basis of the team that was to take Keighley to Wembley was being shaped. Eighteen months after the Wembley appearance, Keighley got to the top of the single league for the only time in its history. The team stayed there for three glorious weeks, but subsided towards the end of the season and eventually finished 13th.

For three weeks in 1938, Keighley headed the Rugby League. The Keighley News published an appropriate cartoon.

*24 years old, **Joe Sherburn** was the first of the 1937 Cup Final team to join Keighley on 14th September 1932. Born in Hull, he had previously played for York and Halifax where the previous season he had scored 35 goals and five tries in thirty appearances. Sherburn, a goal-kicking wing three-quarter, became a very important member of the Keighley team and for the first three seasons with Keighley he topped the club's points scorers. In fact the 1934/35 season became a record setting one for him, for he scored a total of 218 points, breaking his own record of 182 points set the previous season, which, in turn, had broken Bob Walker's 1906/07 tally of 169 points. Sherburn's 1934/35 record was helped by the fact that he scored 30 tries in the season, a record which stood for almost 50 years until it was beaten in the 1993/94 season by Nick Pinkney. In his time at Keighley, Sherburn's abilities were recognised by the county selectors and he played on four occasions for Yorkshire. The war effectively ended Sherburn's career with Keighley after 270 games in which he kicked 221 goals and 115 tries, including scoring four tries in a match twice and two hat tricks..*

This cigarette card featuring Joe Sherburn was no. 47 in a 1935 set of 'Football Caricatures' issued by the manufacturers Ogden

***Dai Davies** was another player recruited by Keighley from the Huddersfield club and another Welshman to boot. He had been born in Glamorgan, and played with Neath before joining the ranks to "go north" with Broughton Rangers, then Warrington before moving on to Huddersfield and subsequently Keighley. Davies joined Keighley on 15th August 1936, having already played in three Challenge Cup Finals, first in 1928 with Warrington when they lost to Swinton at Central Park, Wigan, then again with Warrington when they lost at Wembley to Huddersfield in 1933 and finally in 1935, again at Wembley, this time with Huddersfield when they were beaten by Castleford. When he played in the 1937 Challenge Cup Final with Keighley, it was to be his 4th Cup Final appearance, every time on the losing side. Dai Davies had represented Glamorgan and Monmouthshire on several occasions, the Northern League XIII against the Australians twice, Other Nationalities against England once, and Wales against both England and Australia. Davies had vast experience, and with him also playing in the crucial scrum-half berth it was not at all surprising that he should be appointed team captain. It was no doubt also useful to have a Welshman in charge of a team containing no less than eight players from the Principality. Davies had a very short stay with Keighley. His transfer from Huddersfield in August 1936 had cost the club £200, and on 20th May 1937 he was put on the transfer list at an asking price of £125, having played just 35 games, scoring 12 tries and kicking one goal in his brief career at Keighley.*

Keighley's Wembley year

Keighley's only Wembley appearance came at the end of a season that was otherwise not particularly outstanding - 19 games won out of 38. But the Challenge Cup run caught the imagination of the town, and an estimated 9,000 people - along with 1,000 cases of bottled beer - travelled from Keighley station in 16 special trains. Sixty years ago, this was the only viable way for the majority of supporters to travel to London. The final was played at Wembley four days before the Coronation of King George VI, so Keighley's population had two excuses to celebrate. Unfortunately, the side couldn't deliver a win and actually bring the Cup home. The *Keighley News* remarked that this was *"a disappointing end to a run that was nothing short of miraculous."* Reports of the match were printed on pages 5 and 6 - in those days there was no such thing as front page headlines, as the first page of any newspaper was reserved for adverts.

The road to Wembley was certainly tough. To get through the first round, Keighley had to record their first-ever win at Hunslet, which they did, by a 5-2 margin (a try by Lloyd, a goal by Herbert) in front of 10,000 spectators. Broughton Rangers were despatched 11-5 at Lawkholme in the second round, watched by 8,500 who paid £454 for the privilege. Davies, Lloyd and Parker scored tries, and Herbert kicked a goal. A trip to Liverpool Stanley produced a 7-2 win (try: Talbot, 2 goals: Sherburn) before a couple of epic encounters against Wakefield in the semi-final. The first, at Headingley, saw a 0-0 stalemate watched by 40,034, before Keighley snatched the replay at Fartown, Huddersfield, by 5 points to 3 with a Bevan try and Sherburn goal. Despite only eight points in two semi-final games, both were said to have been 'thrillers' by a contemporary Wakefield supporter.

The Final was watched by 47,699 people who paid a total of £6,540 for the privilege. Any neutrals would probably not have been impressed, as Keighley faded early and their tactics for containing Widnes's star players didn't work. The Lancashire side's half-backs Shannon and McCue, and the loose forward Millington, ran the show. Keighley's pack won plenty of possession, but were otherwise ineffective. Halves Bevan and Davies were disappointing, kicking too much and neglecting the wings Sherburn and Lloyd. When Keighley's threequarters did get some ball, they provided the best passing movements of a fairly drab game. Widnes scored first after seven minutes through Shannon after a pass that some thought was suspiciously forward, and then McCue's interception try gave the Lancashire side an 8-0 half-time lead. A Sherburn penalty reduced the deficit to six points, and Keighley had their best period of the match in the first 20 minutes of the second half, but Widnes posted two more tries, by Barber and McCue, for an unassailable 18-2 lead.

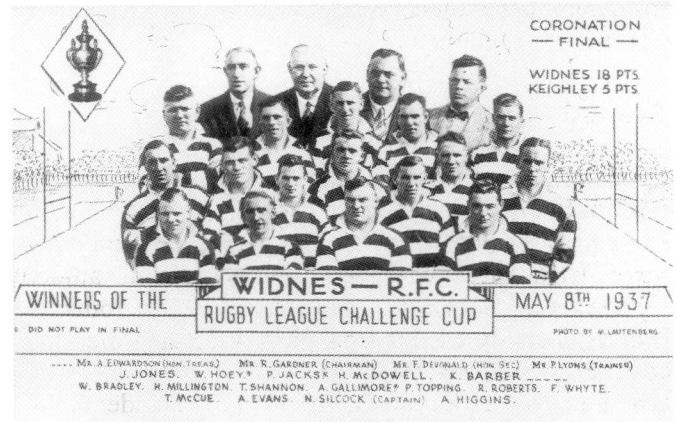

Keighley's Wembley opponents in 1937

The Wembley dream fulfilled: postcard of the Keighley team, published by the Yorkshire Post

KEIGHLEY R.L.F.C.   RESULTS & SCORERS   SEASON 1936-37

Date	Opponents	H/A	Comp	Result	Tries	Goals
Aug-29	Waskefield T	H	RL	L11-25	Orchard (2), Sherburn	D.Davies
Sep-05	Halifax	A	RL	L5-9	T.Davies	T.Davies
Sep-12	Dewsbury	A	YC	L0-8		
Sep-16	Huddersfield	A	RL	L11-20	Talbot, D.Davies, Sherburn	Herbert
Sep-19	Bradford N	H	RL	W12-6	Sherburn, Gill	Bowkett (3)
Sep-26	Leeds	A	RL	W18-15	D.Davies, Sherburn	Bowkett (6)
Sep-29	Featherstone R	A	RL	W17-8	D.Davies, Bevan, Sherburn	Bowkett (3), Phelps
Oct-03	Hull	H	RL	W15-0	D.Davies, Sherburn, Mason	Bowkett (3)
Oct-10	Batley	H	RL	L11-19	McGoun, Lloyd, Orchard	Bowkett
Oct-17	Oldham	A	RL	L2-20		Bowkett
Oct-24	Bramley	H	RL	W8-3	Sherburn, Bevan	Bowkett
Oct-31	Castleford	A	RL	L0-4		
Nov-07	Barrow	A	RL	W8-2	Mason, Bevan	Herbert
Nov-14	Hunslet	H	RL	W13-7	Gill (2), Phelps	Traill (2)
Nov-21	Hull K.R.	A	RL	L2-7		Bowkett
Nov-28	Featherstone R	H	RL	W33-5	Sherburn (4), D.Davies (2) Talbot, Traill, Lloyd	Traill (2), Mason
Dec-05	Warrington	A	RL	L4-10		Sherburn (2)
Dec-12	Halifax	H	RL	W6-0	Sherburn, Talbot	
Dec-19	Hull	A	RL	L5-17	Halliday	Bowkett
Dec-25	Barrow	H	RL	W17-11	Sherburn, Traill, Mason	Bowkett (3), Mason
Dec-26	Newcastle	A	RL	W24-13	Sherburn (2), Lloyd, Phelps Halliday, D.Davies	Sherburn (2), Traill
Jan-02	Wakefield T	A	RL	L3-9	Lloyd	
Jan-09	Castleford	H	RL	L7-10	Lloyd	Sherburn, Herbert
Jan-16	Swinton	A	RL	L2-10		Herbert
Jan-23	Swinton	H	RL	W16-3	Bevan (2), Lloyd, D.Davies	Sherburn (2)
Jan-30	Hunslet	A	RL	L0-8		
Feb-06	Oldham	H	RL	W13-7	Gill, Mason, Sherburn	Herbert, Sherburn
Feb-13	Hunslet	A	RLC	W5-2	Lloyd	Herbert
Feb-20	Dewsbury	A	RL	L0-3		
Feb-27	Broughton R	H	RLC	W11-5	D.Davies, Lloyd, Parker	Herbert
Mar-06	York	A	RL	L6-8	Sherburn, Lloyd	
Mar-13	Liverpool Stanley	A	RLC	W7-2	Talbot	Sherburn (2)
Mar-20	Huddersfield	H	RL	W13-5	Talbot, Bevan, D.Davies	Lloyd, Sherburn
Mar-26	Bradford N	A	RL	L5-8	Bevan	Bowkett
Mar-27	Hull K.R.	H	RL	W25-6	Sherburn (2), D.Davies (2) Lloyd	Sherburn (5)
Mar-29	Leeds	H	RL	L2-12		Bowkett
Mar-30	York	H	RL	W17-11	Bevan (2), Sherburn (2), Gill	Sherburn
Apr-03	Wakefield T	N*	RLC	D0-0		
Apr-07	Wakefield T	N*	RLC	W5-3	Bevan	Sherburn
Apr-10	Warrington	H	RL	L3-11	Parker	
Apr-13	Newcastle	H	RL	W22-15	Lloyd (3), Sherburn (2), Parker	Sherburn (2)
Apr-20	Dewsbury	H	RL	W27-7	Parker (3), Lloyd, Sherburn Traill, Mason	Sherburn (3)
Apr-24	Batley	A	RL	L3-18	Bowkett	
Apr-26	Bramley	A	RL	W9-4	K.Davies, Parker, Jones	
May-08	Widnes	N*	RLC	L5-18	Lloyd	Sherburn

*Cup Semi-final played at Headingley, Leeds, replay at Fartown, Huddersfield
*Cup Final played at Wembley

The Wembley season

Lloyd's try four minutes from the end was mere consolation. Keighley perhaps lacked big-match experience and never really used the advantage they had in pace. The *Daily Express* correspondent pronounced *"a nervous Keighley were beaten by imperturbable Widnes in the first half-hour."* The match was broadcast live on radio (all the match in the north, second half only on national), with commentary by Lance Todd (the New Zealander whose name now adorns the final's man-of-the-match trophy) and Hubert Bateman.

An interesting feature of various celebrations in the days following the Final was a Coronation Eve dance at the Municipal Hall, where players and officials of both Keighley Rugby League Club and Keighlians Rugby Union Club rubbed shoulders. I hope no-one told Twickenham!

Top scorer for the club that season was Joe Sherburn, with 25 goals and 24 tries (122 points) in 42 appearances. Financially, the season was good for the club, with home league gates averaging over £200.

Fleeting post-war glories

The decade and a half following the Second World War was a golden one for Rugby League in general, with huge attendances and massive interest. Keighley attracted relatively big crowds throughout the period, and supporters saw some very talented players at Lawkholme Lane, as well as experiencing some good times. When Chris Brereton was player-coach in 1949-50, the team won 17 out of the last 18 league games of the season, a record unparalleled by Keighley in the single league. Two seasons later, the side reached the Yorkshire Cup Final, beating Castleford, Halifax and Hunslet on the way, but then losing 3-17 to Wakefield. Best league season of the fifties was 1958-59, when the team finished 15th out of 30 clubs, with players of the class of Terry Hollindrake, Ted Verrenkamp, Jim Bardgett, Peter Frain, Derek Hallas and Joe Phillips.

1962-63 saw the re-introduction of two divisions. The first experiment in this direction had lasted three seasons; this one made it for just two before club chairmen decided they'd had enough of it. For the weaker clubs, it meant the

Ted Spillane, or "ET" as he was affectionately known, had two spells with Keighley, first joining the club on 15th November 1932 at the age of 25. At that time he was the first colonial player to have been signed by the club. Spillane was a New Zealander who had represented his country twice and played three times for the South Island against the North Island. He had the spent two and a half years with Wigan before joining Keighley, the transfer fee being £150. Spillane transformed the Keighley team, scoring two tries in his debut match, on both occasions beating three opponents. When he joined the club, Keighley were struggling, and although there had been signs of an improvement it did not actually happen until Spillane came. Just two weeks after his arrival he was appointed captain and coach of the team. Under his guidance the standard of play rose and attendances increased - his debut was witnessed by 4,000 spectators, the best of the season - with the result than money flowed in, enabling ground improvements and the construction of a wooden stand. In Spillane's first season Keighley won 18 games, 16 of them after his arrival. Spillane left Keighley for arch rivals Bradford Northern on 28th December 1934, having scored 20 tries and kicked four goals in 56 games. On 20th November 1937, Spillane rejoined Keighley - this time as player coach in succession to Len Bowkett. His second spell was, though, much shorter than the first, for he moved on to Bramley on 23rd August 1938 having played just 17 matches, scoring one try and kicking two goals in that period. Spillane's influence lived on, however, for in November 1938 Keighley, for the first time ever, went to the top of the Rugby League.

Idris Towill was born in Bridgend and captained his local club before joining Huddersfield in 1931. At Huddersfield his achievements included winning the Yorkshire Cup in 1931/32 and appearing at Wembley in the 1935 Challenge Cup Final when they lost to Castleford. He played 94 times for Huddersfield, scoring 20 tries, and gained international recognition for Wales, playing at stand-off in the same match as club mate Len Bowkett in January 1932. On 24th November 1936, Towill was transferred to Keighley for the princely sum of £300 and so became jointly the most expensive player, along with fellow centre threequarter Gwyn Parker, of Keighley's Challenge Cup Final team. Towill was one of the few members of that Challenge Cup team to remain with the club for any length of time; he stayed throughout the war years to register 271 appearances for the club, scoring 55 tries in the process, his biggest tally coming in a match against Rochdale Hornets on 17th December 1938, when he scored four tries in the match. He may not have been a prolific try scorer, but his value to the team was immeasurable. Towill's career with Keighley was to last until injury brought it to an end in April 1946. On 14th May 1946 a benefit match was played, which Towill shared with fellow centre-threequarter Norman Foster.

Joe Flanagan was involved in professional Rugby League for 40 years, first as a player with Keighley, Leeds, Whitehaven and Bramley, then as a referee, and finally as a coach. He started playing with Keighley during the second World War, having graduated from the local amateur league with the St.Anne's team. During that first spell with Keighley, Flanagan gained a Yorkshire Cup Final medal in the team that lost to Bradford Northern in a two-legged affair in the 1943/44 season. In the 1947/48 season, Keighley sold Flanagan to Leeds for a then record club fee of £1,000, and during his one season stay with the Headingley club he was chosen to play for Yorkshire. Unfortunately, an injury picked up in the Yorkshire Cup Final prevented him from representing his county. Flanagan joined Whitehaven on that club's formation at the beginning of the 1948/49 season and scored their first points with a goal. With travelling proving troublesome, Flanagan returned to Keighley in early 1949 and played three further seasons at Lawkholme before moving finally to Bramley. After his playing days came to an end, Flanagan took up refereeing, firstly within the amateur leagues but then progressing to the professional game and refereed a match between Wakefield and the New Zealand touring team, among others.

February 1939 team v. Featherstone. Back: Innes, McDonald, Harris, Fuller, Evans, Walton, Thonber, Sherburn. Front: Farrington, Towill, Jenkins, Horrod, Foster

3rd August 1946 v. Batley. Back: J. Flanagan, Stringer, Childs, Fell, McManus, Bailey, Grace. Front: Elias, Mills, Burnett, Barrett, Holmes, Ward

Chris Brereton was a prop forward of great stature, the keystone round which the Keighley pack of the late 40s and early 50s was built. He had originally been with Halifax, but joined Leeds in late 1946 and had a quite successful period with the Headingley club, which included an appearance in the 1947 Challenge Cup Final at Wembley, before joining Keighley. It was a fearsome Keighley pack that Brereton led, and it was reputed to have been fed on raw meat before the Challenge Cup tie with Workington in 1950. The pack also included Joe Britton, Alex Mulhall and Ivor Davies, and, whatever they were actually fed on, they beat the more fancied Workington in both legs of the tie. In all, Brereton played 76 times for Keighley, scoring 12 tries, before his departure in 1952.

Lawkholme Lane, 30th August 1949. Keighley v. Hunslet. Back: Powles, J. Flanagan, D. Thornton, C. Brereton, J. Britton, E. Hudson, I. Mulhall. Front: L. Ward, F. Barrett, E. Redman, J.J. Mills, Buckley, M. Delloyd

Terry Hollindrake, Keighley's points machine of the 1950's and a Great Britain international, often credits his success to the example set by **Len Ward**. Ward, who had been born in Castleford, preceded Hollindrake by five or six seasons, having joined Keighley during the 1944/45 season. He had moved to Keighley in his teens and played with Keighley Albion and Huddersfield's "A" team before turning professional with the Keighley club. Ward went on to play 336 times for Keighley, representing Yorkshire on five occasions between May 1949 and November 1951. His last appearance for his county was against the New Zealand tourists at Belle Vue, Wakefield. Ward's only other honour was a runners-up medal earned with Keighley in the 1951 Yorkshire Cup Final. It was mainly on the wing that Ward made his name, scoring 139 tries in his career and it was his trademark side-step which Hollindrake emulated with so much success. On his retirement from playing, Ward continued his association with the Keighley club by being retained in a coaching capacity with the "A" Team.

Team and officials leaving for an away Challenge Cup match at Workington in February 1950, which Keighley won 5-0. At back (l. to r.): T. Bell, E. Halls, Bedford, Creesey, Ivill, Brereton, P. Beadman, Callaghan, Sykes, Mills, F. Taylor, K. Davies, Watson, J. Smith. Front: Barrett, Britton, Delloyd, D. Jenkins

loss of attractive derbies - and a big crowd - against top clubs in their county, while for every club it meant fewer fixtures. But as in 1902-3, Keighley won promotion at the first attempt - though they were promptly relegated again. The promotion-winning team of the sixties included stars like Roy Bleasby, Garfield Owen, Ken Pye, Roy Sabine, Alf Barron, Dave Worthy, Geoff Crewdson, Albert Eyre, Mel Smith and Brian Todd. Owen kicked 128 goals in 1962-63, beating Joe Phillips' previous record.

Terry Hollindrake has the distinction of being the only Keighley born player to represent Great Britain. That was in 1955 at Headingley against New Zealand when he took the place of the legendary Billy Boston. A product of Keighley Albion, Terry joined Keighley in December 1951 and remained with the club, National Service curtailing his career somewhat, until he was controversially transferred to Hull F.C. in October 1960 for a then club record £6,000. In his original contract, on joining Keighley, Terry was due to receive £175 after six first team appearances and £50 if he played for Yorkshire. Chairman John Smallwood subsequently gave him a new contract which offered Terry £250 after six first team games, £500 if he played for Yorkshire and £1,000 if he played for Great Britain. At the time, of course, Mr.Smallwood did not know Terry would do all three! Early in the 1959-60 season Terry, a strong, speedy wing-threequarter (having learned many of the skills from Len Ward) and prolific goal kicker, overtook the then record 787 points in a career which had been set by Joe Sherburn in the thirties, and he went on to be the first Keighley player to pass the 1,000 points mark. He regards 1955-56 as his best season, when he played outside centre Alan Taylor. From Hull, Terry moved on to Bramley, and in 1968 he returned to amateur rugby in Keighley with the Shamrocks before, once again, taking up the professional game with Keighley in the 1969/70 season. It is ironic that his first and last professional games were for Keighley's "A" team against Bramley, but almost 20 years apart.

The team against Hunslet at Lawkholme 0n 25th October 1952. Back: T. Devanney, P. Callaghan, K. Harden, J. James, K. Holbrook, I. Davies, P. Riley. Front: E. Prescott, P. Anson, H. Palin, W. Ivill, L. Ward, J. Rock

The side for a Trevor Foster benefit game against Bradford Northern in August 1955. Back: A. Traill, A. Grice, K. Holbrook, R. Raines, J. Bardgett, T. Devanney. Seated: T.Hollindrake, L. Ward, T. Verenkamp, A, Taylor, D. Smith. Kneeling: N. Black, A. Rowlands

John Smallwood, Keighley's Chairman at the time of **Roy Sabine**'s joining Keighley in September 1958, tells the story of Sabine's capture from under the noses of Halifax. Sabine had been getting good reports, in the amateur ranks, in the Yorkshire Sports newspaper, and Bill Shreeve, a Keighley player at the time, mentioned to Mr. Smallwood that a young lad living in the same street as himself was worth looking at. Smallwood needed no further prompting and quickly arranged a meeting with Sabine, who informed the Keighley chairman that he had signed for trials with Halifax and that he was asking £600 for his signature. Mr. Smallwood told Sabine that Keighley would pay him that if he proved his ability. The rest, as they say, is history.

Sabine signed for Keighley, making his debut at home to Castleford on 27th September 1958 and scoring a try in the match. His second match was at Halifax and Sabine showed the Thrum Hall club what they had missed by scoring a hat trick of tries in Keighley's 22-9 victory. In eight seasons with Keighley, playing normally in the stand off position but occasionally in the centre berth, Sabine played in 175 matches, scoring 46 tries and making two appearances for Yorkshire in 1963, one against the Australian tourists. As a player Sabine left Keighley in 1966, but he returned as coach in August 1975 and took the team to that famous Challenge Cup semi-final against St. Helens at Fartown the following year. His coaching stint at Keighley ended in October 1977.

KEIGHLEY R.L.F.C. RESULTS & SCORERS SEASON 1974-75

Date	Opponents	H/A	Comp	Result	Tries	Goals	Drop Goals
Aug-25	Salford	H	D1	W11-7	Roe	Jefferson (4)	
Aug-31	Leeds	A	YC	L5-16	Garbett	Jefferson	
Sep-08	Halifax	A	D1	W25-8	Sutcliffe (3), Leek, Illingworth	Jefferson (5)	
Sep-15	Castleford	H	D1	W15-14	Sutcliffe, Roe, Valentine	Sutcliffe (3)	
Sep-17	Hull	A	FT	L2-12		Orr	
Sep-21	Bramley	A	D1	W19-15	Wilkes, Stenton, Roe	Orr (5)	
Sep-29	Halifax	A	JP	W13-11	Wilkes	Orr (5)	
Oct-02	Salford	A	D1	L2-45		Orr	
Oct-06	Wakefield T	H	D1	L7-15	Garbett	Orr (2)	
Oct-11	St.Helens	A	D1	L7-33	Loxton	Orr (2)	
Oct-19	Warrington	H	D1	L12-13	O'Brien, Brosnan	Garbett (3)	
Oct-30	Wakefield T	A	D1	L13-20	Orr (2), Johnson	Orr (2)	
Nov-03	Leeds	H	D1	L12-28	Loxton	Jefferson (4)	Jefferson
Nov-10	Leeds	H	JP	L4-39		Orr (2)	
Nov-17	York	A	D1	W11-9	Brosnan, Valentine	Orr (2)	Orr
Nov-24	Dewsbury	H	D1	W7-5	Roe	Orr (2)	
Dec-01	Rochdale H	A	D1	W10-5	Burke (2)	Orr (2)	
Dec-08	Wigan	H	D1	L17-20	Garbett, Obst, Orr	Orr (4)	
Dec-15	Dewsbury	A	D1	W8-4	Wilkes, Loxton	Orr	
Dec-21	Leeds	A	D1	L9-24	Raper	Obst (3)	
Jan-05	Bradford N	H	D1	L9-12	Burke	Orr (3)	
Jan-12	St.Helens	H	D1	L5-13	Garbett	Orr	
Jan-19	Featherstone R	A	D1	L10-15	Roe, Valentine	Orr (2)	
Jan-26	Rochdale H	H	D1	W14-5	Johnson, Gallacher	Orr (3), Sutcliffe	
Feb-09	York	A	RLC	L9-26	Wilkes	Orr (3)	
Feb-16	Widnes	H	D1	L5-10	Fisher	Orr	
Mar-02	Widnes	A	D1	L0-8			
Mar-09	Halifax	H	D1	L9-15	Valentine	Orr (3)	
Mar-14	Castleford	A	D1	L8-13	Garbett, Johnson	Garbett	
Mar-23	Featherstone R	H	D1	W12-2	Sabine (2)	Jefferson (3)	
Mar-30	Bradford N	A	D1	W14-5	Garbett, Raistrick, Jickells	Jefferson (2)	Jefferson
Apr-01	York	H	D1	W6-2		Jefferson (3)	
Apr-11	Bramley	H	D1	W11-3	Loxton, Johnson	Jefferson (2)	Jefferson
Apr-13	Warrington	A	D1	L7-16	Garforth	Jefferson (2)	
Apr-19	Wigan	A	D1	L5-40	Jickells	Garbett	
Apr-27	Dewsbury	A	PT	W9-8	Loxton	Jefferson (3)	
Apr-30	Hull K.R.	A	PT	L10-29	Johnson, Stephenson	Clarkson (2)	

The only season when Keighley stayed in the top division after promotion, with 13 wins in 30 games. They were relegated the season after. Notable scalps included Halifax and Castleford.

Derek Hallas was John Smallwood's first signing for Keighley after he became chairman of the board of directors in 1953. Mr. Smallwood once explained that Hallas was signed in the chief scout's living room on a very foggy night. Hallas had played Rugby Union with the Roundhay club before joining Keighley for a signing on fee of £400, which was a large figure for a player with little, if any, Rugby League experience. Hallas made his debut against Dewsbury at Lawkholme Lane on 2nd January 1954, scoring two tries for his new club. It is ironic that his final game for Keighley was also against Dewsbury, but this time at Crown Flatt, on 27th December 1958, before he was transferred to the Parramatta club in Australia. Having played five years for Keighley, Hallas's transfer to Parramatta cost his new club £4,000 - a good return for the Keighley club for the original investment. Hallas played in an impressive back division for much of the time, partnering David Smith at centre, with Roy Bleasby and Terry Hollindrake or Len Ward on the wings, Bert Cook, Peter Frain, Neville Black or Joe Phillips at full back and Ted Verrenkamp and Alfie Barron at half back. Hallas' skills in the centre position were recognised by the county selectors, who chose him for two Yorkshire matches and he represented England Services against the French Services team. For Keighley, Hallas made 171 appearances, scoring 68 tries and 6 goals.

Geoff Crewdson was one of only four Keighley players to have toured with the Great Britain team. He was a huge man by any standards and a special shirt had to be made for the tour party to fit his 17 stone frame. Geoff had joined Keighley at the age of 17 years, having formerly been associated with Leeds juniors, and made his debut as a loose forward in March 1956. He had the distinction of playing in Keighley's 1960/61 Yorkshire Cup Semi-Final, albeit losing 5-4 to the star studded Wakefield Trinity team. In 1965, Geoff was moved to the front of the scrum and relished in the role. It was no surprise that honours beckoned and in the 1965/66 season he was selected as a reserve for both Yorkshire and Great Britain. On 23rd March 1966 the squad to tour Australia was announced and it included Geoff Crewdson. Although he did not appear in the Test team on tour, he did play in 13 tour games. The last of Geoff's 288 games for Keighley was on 26th October 1968 against Blackpool Borough. He subsequently played for Hunslet and, at the age of 37, appeared against his former club at Elland Road Greyhound Stadium in March 1974.

The Keighley side in a cup-tie against Oldham in February 1964. Back (left to right): Mel Smith, Terry O'Brien, Albert Bloomfield, Brian Wright, Geoff Crewdson, Albert Eyre, Barrie Anderson. Front: Brian Daniel, Peter Frain, Peter Reilly, Garfield Owen, Alan Edwards, Ken Pye (photo: Keighley News)

Joe Phillips came from Wellington, New Zealand, and joined Keighley in January 1957 after six successful years with arch rivals Bradford Northern. Back home in New Zealand, Phillips had an All Black trial and he joined Northern in 1950 making his debut at York on 30th September. For Northern, Phillips kicked 699 goals and scored 49 tries - a total of 1,545 points. During his time at Bradford, Phillips made four appearances for the Other Nationalities and also played for Australasia against Great Britain in 1951. For Keighley, Phillips made his debut on 2nd February 1957 and the following season set a club record of 261 points in the season with 111 goals and 13 tries. Those 13 tries from the full back position were a club record which stood until the 1994/95 season when Andre Stoop scored 14 tries from that position. After three seasons with Keighley, Phillips retired and became successful in business. When the Bradford Northern club folded in January 1964, Phillips became the first chairman of the reborn Northern (now Bradford Bulls!) and his efforts were rewarded when the new club kicked off in August 1964 with a crowd of 14,500 spectators at Odsal for the first game of the new club.

Colin Evans was one of the few ex-Rugby Union scrum halves to have made a notably successful career as a Rugby League scrum half. In his Rugby Union career with Pontypool, Evans was capped by Wales when he made his one and only appearance against England in 1960. Within two weeks of achieving that honour, he joined Leeds R.L.F.C., making his debut against Doncaster on 6th February 1960. After 140 appearances for Leeds, which included a Championship Final winning appearance alongside Lewis Jones against Warrington in 1961, Evans was surprisingly transferred to York in January 1964, before ending his career with Keighley. It was in October 1966 that Evans joined Keighley, making his debut against Halifax at Thrum Hall on the 8th of that month. A popular player with the Keighley fans, Evans played 165 games before retiring to the coaching staff in 1972.

Roy Bleasby came into the Keighley team in the fifties and blossomed alongside the likes of Derek Hallas, David Smith, Alan Taylor, Joe Phillips and the legendary Terry Hollindrake. Indeed, as well as playing alongside Hollindrake, Bleasby fought Hollindrake for the left wing spot, so you can judge Bleasby's value to the team by the fact that Hollindrake was moved in field to cater for him. Bleasby made his debut in the first team at Castleford on 27th September 1952 and proceeded to play nine full seasons for the club before retiring at the end of the 1962/63 season. That season was a fateful one for Bleasby, for the big freeze, which prevented play for the whole of January and February, caused him to miss out on a benefit match. He missed one full season due to National Service and, but for his duty to the nation, must surely have passed the magic 300 appearances in his career. As it was, he managed 229 matches for Keighley, scoring 117 tries along the way. It was a notable achievement for Bleasby, despite having such skilful players as Hallas, Smith and Hollindrake in the side, that for three successive seasons he was Keighley's leading try scorer.

Geoff Beadnall, Keighley's scout, tipped off the Keighley Board about **Albert Eyre**, who was playing schoolboy and junior rugby, but both Hunslet and Leeds were also keen to sign him. No club could sign Eyre until he was 16 years old and his 16th birthday happened to be on a Sunday. John Smallwood, Keighley's Chairman in 1959, relates the circumstances surrounding Eyre's capture. "We picked Albert up on the Saturday morning, which happened to be Keighley Gala day, brought him to Keighley and asked Fred Anderson, the young stand off, to look after him at the gala. Albert signed in Keighley at five minutes past midnight and we then drove him back to his home in Hunslet, where both Leeds and Hunslet were waiting. They were none too pleased when they found out we had signed him for Keighley." Eyre was to prove to be an inspired capture for the Keighley club and a firm favourite with the Keighley supporters. Eyre began his career as a centre three-quarter, but then developed into a first rate back row forward. In all, Eyre made 192 appearances, scoring 28 tries, in seven seasons with Keighley before eventually joining his brother Kenneth at Leeds in August 1967. His career with Leeds was highlighted by an appearance in the famous "water splash" Challenge Cup Final at Wembley in 1968 which Leeds won courtesy of that famous missed goal kick from in front of the posts with the last kick of the match by Wakefield Trinity's Don Fox.

Road to oblivion - and rescue

The seventies began promisingly, with sixth place in a single league the best since 1909-10. They slumped to 26th the year after, before the Rugby League's third foray into a two divisional system. In 1973-74, Keighley achieved a hat-trick of promotions and then, for the one and only season, stayed in the top division of Rugby League on merit, finishing 11th. Relegation followed the season after, and the club stayed in the second tier for fifteen years, until a third division was set up for season 1991-2, the first year of the Cougars.

The financial mess the club was in by 1987 and the recent poor playing records (the club finished in the bottom six for three consecutive seasons) were reflected in dwindling crowds. In March of that year, as the directors were fighting tax demands and planning a move to Marley, Keighley hosted successive all-time low attendances - 322 against Mansfield Marksmen in March, 216 to watch Fulham three weeks later. Keighley finished that season bottom of Division 2 - their worst-ever season. In 1919-20, when they also finished bottom of the league, there were only 25 professional clubs. Now they were below everyone. *"Rock bottom - and waiting for a miracle,"* proclaimed the *Keighley News*. The sale of the ground to the Yorkshire Co-op got rid of the immediate problem, and the performance of the team could once again be the focal point. In the following four seasons, the side finished eighth (twice), nineteenth and thirteenth in the second division. Then came the Cougars.

Brian Jefferson was the master as far as kicking the ball was concerned. His goal kicking won many a match for Keighley and his drop goals demoralised the opposition on many occasions. For most of Jefferson's days the drop goal was worth 2 points and therefore had a far greater influence on the match than those of today. It is a measure of his ability to kick drop goals from almost any angle that he kicked 34 in the 1973/74 season alone. His goal kicking was not the only skill he commanded. His tactical kicking kept the opposition penned back inside their own territory and he scored a few tries - 64 in his career with Keighley. Jefferson was originally a Rugby Union player with Moortown, where he had won Yorkshire County representative honours, but in November 1965 a thirteen season Rugby League career began with Keighley. Jefferson's 967 goals and 2,116 points, amassed in 300 games between 1965 and 1977, are a career record for the Keighley club and it is therefore not surprising that he won representative honours with Yorkshire County, captaining the team twice, and a lone appearance for England. The 66 points Jefferson scored for Yorkshire comprised 30 goals and 3 tries. A knee operation brought Jefferson's playing career to an end in November 1977, but he maintained his association with Keighley by taking up the reins as a coach and setting up a Colts team which he was eventually to take to the Halifax club when the Keighley board decided it was no longer viable at Lawkholme.

Paul Moses started and finished his professional career at Keighley, with a brief three year spell at Halifax in between. In the early days it was with the Colts that Paul first became connected with the Keighley club, but when the Colts team folded and went lock, stock and barrel to Halifax, Paul went with them. Halifax was effectively where Paul learned his trade, making his debut in November 1981 but reaching the top level in the 1983/84 season, just before the influx of overseas players who took Halifax to the Championship and the Challenge Cup Final. Halifax's loss, though, was Keighley's gain, and Paul returned to his home town club in December 1984, firstly on loan, then in a permanent deal which in which he saw action over 10 seasons, eventually earning himself a benefit year. Originally a scrum-half, Paul was latterly converted to the hooking role, but in both capacities he served the club well. In all, Paul made 205 appearance for the club scoring 35 tries, 17 goals and a remarkable 37 drop-goals. He was one of those players who stuck with the team when they were at rock bottom in the late 80s, but was lucky enough to be still involved in the Cougar era and enjoyed just a small part of the glory when the 3rd Division Championship was won in the 1992/93 season. With age catching up with him (although to look at him you'd think he was still in his teens), Paul joined the coaching staff at Keighley before moving back into the amateur ranks in the local league.

John Burke was another of Keighley's crowd pleasers who had connections with the Leeds club. Burke had five seasons with Leeds, making his debut in October 1967, which included a winning Yorkshire Cup Final appearance in 1970 and a losing Challenge Cup Final appearance at Wembley in 1971. In August 1972, Burke was transferred to Keighley and proceeded to make a prop forward position his own for four seasons. His robust style of play and occasional indiscretions drew the attention of the match officials, and subsequent retribution from the disciplinary committee limited his Keighley career to 104 appearances and eight tries before he departed in 1976.

1982-83 season. Back: David Moll, Gary Hodgson, Les Sellers, Alex Kalinowski, Terry Brearley, Derek Arnold, Mick Hawksworth. Front: Andy Scanlon, Kevin Morgan, Colin Robinson, Graham Beale, Trevor Briggs, Sam Illingworth

The romance of Lawkholme Lane

Rugby was first played at the present Lawkholme Lane ground on September 19th 1885, a friendly made up of two informal teams captained by Fould and Haigh. Keighley Rugby Club had been formed nine years earlier, and played on a field in the Lawkholme area before moving to Dalton Lane, opposite the Beeches. The impetus for a move to a new ground in 1885 was provided by Keighley Cricket Club, who bought land from the Duke of Devonshire to provide facilities for themselves and the rugby club. A sum of £250 was paid to the cricket club for the costs they incurred, and the rugby club continued to pay a rental until 1933, when the leasehold was bought.

The first competitive game at the new ground was on Saturday 3rd October 1885, when visitors Liversedge won quite comfortably. The match had been kicked off by Keighley's captain William 'Pusher' Yiend, who went on to play for England, though this was after he left the Keighley club. For the next fifteen years, Keighley continued to play the original code of rugby, missing out on the original 1895 breakaway of leading clubs in Yorkshire and Lancashire. In 1900, though, following the trend of clubs to want to pay players to compensate them for not working on Saturday afternoons, Keighley applied to join the Northern Union, and were accepted into the fold on June 12th of that year. Sowerby Bridge were the first league visitors to Lawkholme Lane, graciously losing 5-0 before a decent crowd of about 2,000. There was no protection for spectators from the elements for another three decades, and in 1921 the ground was described as *"the poorest in the league."* The playing area was below maximum dimensions, and Keighley often had difficulty in persuading Lancashire sides onto their fixture list in the days when inter-county club games were arranged by mutual consent.

Later in the season, a second round cup game against York drew a crowd of over 5,000, who paid at least sixpence each, the equivalent of about £6 today. The potential for big crowds at Lawkholme was obvious, given a successful team.

Lawkholme Lane has always been a scenic ground, perhaps the best in the league. The Australian tourists of 1921 certainly reckoned it was the winner for beautiful surroundings. *Keighley News* writer in the fifties, C. Senior, enthused: *"the ground is certainly charming for it*

The familiar landmark of the Lawkholme clock forms a backdrop to Derek Arnold as he sprints clear in a game against Hunslet on 25th September 1983. Gary Hodgson is in support, while the player behind Arnold is Peter Roe, who later became Keighley's coach for two separate periods

embraces acres and acres of steep picturesque hillside stretching from the River Aire right up to the fringe of the famous Ilkley Moors... the onlooker from 'Spion Kop' (town end terrace) *has, indeed, often found more enchantment in the distant view beyond than in the displays of his team!"*

Until 1925, the teams actually changed in the town itself, in primitive accommodation behind the "King's Arms" on Church Green. Fifteen minutes before kick-off, two horse-drawn charabancs (one for each team) would turn up, with the referee and touch judges having a separate cab. The unusual procession would then set off along Skipton Road, turn down Cavendish Street, and onto Lawkholme Lane, their eventual arrival at the ground always ensuring a rapturous welcome. The return journey, however, could become something of a nightmare for the opposition, especially if they'd won, with a mile of hostile territory to negotiate. The referee, too, sometimes found it prudent to organise alternative, less public, transport, after the game.

Lawkholme was transformed after the end of the 1932-33 season, when the ambitions of chairman J.W. Booth and secretary Norman Harrison, after several notable player signings, were directed to improving the ground. The open stand, which had been the only area approaching comfort for spectators, was pulled down, and a new covered stand built in the same place on the side adjoining the cricket ground. On September 9th, it was officially opened by Sir Edwin Airey. At the same time the playing area, which had been one of the narrowest in the Rugby League, was widened. Two

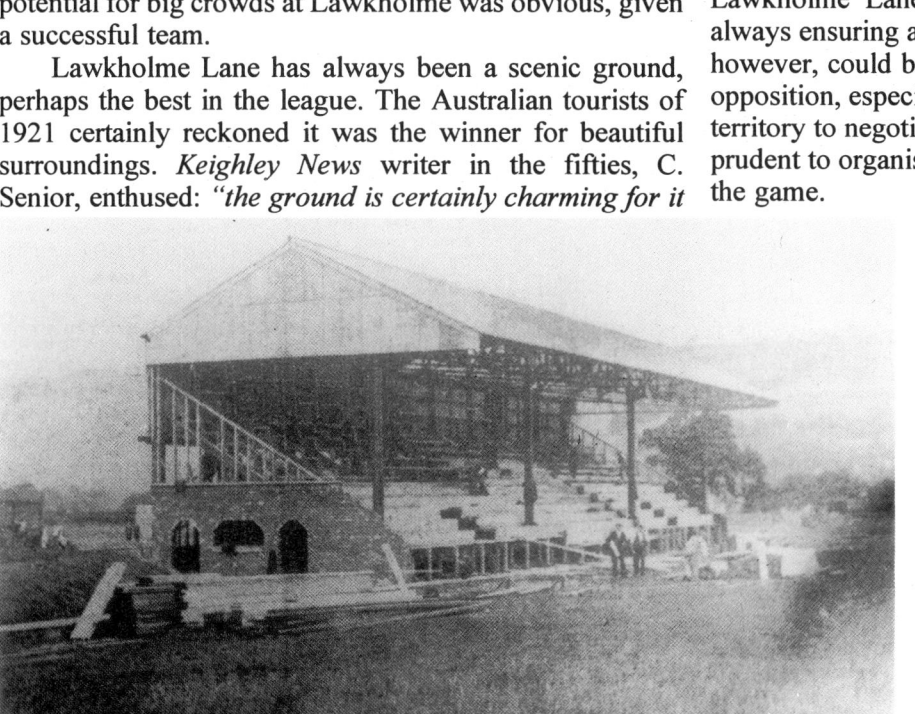

Construction of the grandstand in July 1933

seasons later, cover was provided on the opposite side - this stand became affectionately known as 'The Scrattin' Shed' - and in the late 1940's terracing was built on the town end of the ground. In 1950, *Rugby League Review*, a weekly journal, was able to comment that *"the Lawkholme enclosure is quite a modern up to date stadium."* Perhaps 'stadium' was going slightly over the top, but ground capacity was then an impressive 18,000. In March 1951, a club record crowd of 14,500, paying £1,645, watched Keighley narrowly lose 6-7 to Halifax in the second round of the Challenge Cup.

Above: Lawkholme Lane in 1932 with its lack of cover for spectators. Below: two views of Cougar Park in 1998 (photos: Brian Lund)

John Smallwood became chairman in 1953 and a year later launched an appeal to raise £8,500 to pay for the cost of new dressing rooms (and bath, which was condemned as deplorable) and stand extension. A letter to businesses in the town was angled at their corporate responsibilities: *"The directors of Keighley RLFC are anxious to provide good football for the town - and the men who play and those who watch naturally expect good conditions. The existing dressing rooms are a disgrace... no matter how many you employ, can it be denied that good football in pleasant surroundings provides your employees with healthy relaxation and stimulation for the week's industry?"* Shopkeepers were sent a slightly different version, based on the value of a strong team to the town's image and commerce. Supporters, too, were urged to help: the programme for the game against Huddersfield in February 1954 urged: *"We want more members; we want more shareholders; and we want more donations."*

In October 1961, the club bought the Lawkholme Lane ground from the Duke of Devonshire's estate. Rugby there should have been assured in perpetuity, but, as always, a financial crisis intervened to change that prospect. By the mid-1980's, possibly the worst of all decades for the club, years of neglect and depression had reduced the ground to a sad sight. In the aftermath of the Bradford City fire disaster, sports clubs were forced to look closely at their spectator safety, and Lawkholme Lane was in trouble. The stand was declared unfit by safety officers, and the floodlights condemned as dangerous. At one point, the ground capacity was reduced to a maximum 1,200. In November 1986, with the Inland Revenue and Customs & Excise demanding £37,000, with no money in the kitty for either this or ground improvements, the directors decided on the drastic step of selling the ground. Negotiations with a do-it-yourself retail outfit were well advanced, but planning permission could not be obtained and this idea collapsed. Certainly, if Bradford Council had granted planning permission, Lawkholme would have become a superstore and the club would have moved to the Marley site recently vacated by the town's Rugby Union club. Accountants were called in to stall the tax demands, and the saga rumbled on until, with debts climbing to £150,000, a fairy godmother stepped in. The Yorkshire Co-op agreed to buy the ground and lease it back to the club. Another crisis had been averted at the last minute. The directors had even considered a move to a council-run pitch at Colne, an idea as impractical as the suggested switch to Burnley when another financial crisis gripped the club in 1996. Before that, though, Lawkholme Lane had been transformed into Cougar Park.

Printed in Great Britain
by Amazon

Project Contributors

Martin Kalemba
Rosaline Macauley
Mukami McCrum
Shupikai Mwanza
Justin Ehimen
Ifeoma Omenyima
Ngozi Ebiem
Kamel Elnageh
Amina Kahjobarteh
Mariama Jobarteh
Eva Asante
David Okalo Olwa
Lankey Sesemani
Kobi Cooke
Henry Karaka
Jonathan Ssentamu
Sharon Nalweyiso
Tzaritsa Asante
Hashim Kalyango
Barry Davidson
Heather Robertson

ensuring I honed my craft to capture each story's essence effectively. From exploring different artistic styles to mastering new techniques, I immersed myself in a world of creativity and learning, all to bring these stories to their fullest potential.

This project has been a journey of growth, both personally and artistically, as I have been pushed to new limits and challenged to create with truth and empathy. I pray that these images will light a spark within you, inspiring you to embrace curiosity, joy, and meaningful questions. May you join me in witnessing the beauty and resilience of the human spirit.

Tzaritsa Asante.

A message from the book's illustrator

In illustrating the stories in this book, I found myself deeply immersed in everyone's narrative, recognising the profound uniqueness of their experiences. Whilst there may have been overarching themes running through their stories, it was imperative to honour the distinct essence of each person's identity and ensure that their story was authentically and visually represented.

As I delved into their stories, I realised the importance of fusing their truth with mine. It wasn't just about illustrating their words; it was about infusing their stories with the depth of my understanding and empathy. As an artist, I had to draw on my encounters, emotions, and interpretations to bring their stories to life in a way that resonated with authenticity.

Inspired by the brilliant talent of artists from the African diaspora, I embarked on a journey of self-improvement,

LIVING MEMORY ASSOCIATION

THE WEE MUSEUM

The Living Memory Association uses reminiscence and community history to bring people of all backgrounds and ages together, record memories, save valuable history for the future, increase skills and, above all, create fun and enjoyment.

The Living Memory Association Wee Museum has played a crucial role in bringing An Immigrant's Financial Journey Project to fruition.

HERITAGE LOTTERY FUND

Thriving Beyond Borders has been made possible thanks to the Heritage Fund, which supported the Enkula Wellness Hub project, An Immigrant's Financial Journey. The project "An Immigrant's Financial Journey" focused on African migrants to the UK who have made Scotland home, capturing their heritage and histories in various formats and expressions, highlighting their heritage, transition, and financial experiences. The project has brought together a remarkably diverse range of intergenerational participants aged up to 85, unleashing some heritage gems of creative expression. This book is one form of the various expressions in which we have captured the powerful stories and heritage of African Migrants.

ENKULA WELLNESS HUB C.I.C

This book has been written as part of Enkula Wellness Hub's **"An Immigrant's Financial Journey" Project**, which seeks to capture the heritage of people of African Descent who moved to make Scotland home and their lived experiences of money and life before they moved to Scotland and as they transitioned to make Scotland home.

ENKULA WELLNESS HUB inspires, educates, and enables minoritised communities and supports them in prioritising wellness in all its forms.

VISION: Leave a lasting impact on communities by helping people unlock their full potential through real, relevant, and contemporary wellness programs delivered in an inclusive and culturally conscious manner.

Acknowledgements

Personal Development: You will enhance your leadership and strategic thinking skills, contributing to your professional development.

2. Angel investing and venture capital

High-risk, high-reward investments: Angel investing financially supports small start-ups or entrepreneurs, often in exchange for equity or convertible debt.

How to get involved:

Education and research: Learn about angel investing through courses, workshops, and networking with experienced investors.

Join an angel network: connect with a network of angel investors to find investment opportunities and learn from their experiences.

PS: If you have been investing in your country of origin, backing friends or families, guess what? You may already be an Angel Investor. So don't feel intimidated or feel it's too steep a climb; start where you are.

3. Planning for Tax and Inheritance

To figure out your tax obligations in the UK, it's important to consider things like income, selling assets, and inheritance. Proper planning will help you minimise tax liabilities.

Write your will: Make sure you have a will to protect your assets and distribute them according to your wishes. Writing a will can help you think ahead to setting up trusts and other estate planning hacks that can maximise your assets.

Learning Moment: Leaving a Legacy

When you move to a new country, your dream isn't just to survive but to thrive and leave a solid financial legacy for future generations—ideally, while leaving the world better than you found it.

Please look at these ways to approach it.

1. Board positions and influencing policy: External candidates can be paid to join the boards of various UK organisations, including charities and public bodies. These roles provide pay and give you a unique opportunity to influence policies and decisions.

How to get involved:

Develop skills: Cultivate skills and experience in high demand for board positions, such as financial expertise, strategic planning, and governance. There are also specific resources for Non-Executive Directors (NEDS) and similar roles.

Networking and visibility: Increase your visibility in your professional and community circles by attending industry conferences, joining professional associations, and participating in community events.

Volunteer: Start by volunteering on committees or advisory roles to build your governance experience and network before applying for a paid role.

Potential Impact

Influence policy: Serving on a board allows you to contribute to key decisions shaping industry direction and policy, potentially influencing legislation or public opinion.

However, on the third day of this induction, Tito Lutwa Okello staged a coup d'état that toppled President Milton Obote. As a result, David's plans for Uganda were abruptly halted once again. This disappointed him because he had acquired much knowledge and was ready to make positive changes in the country. So, he returned to working in the health services sector and joined the Capital planning team at Lothian Health Planning and Development. Building St John's Hospital in Livingston early was one of his proudest achievements. Before retiring in 2007, he held different roles, including chairing the West Lothian Community Race Forum and establishing the Black People's Issues section at UNISON.

re-qualifying or finding alternative pathways into their profession.

After navigating through the red tape, David worked for various government departments. He spent 11 years at West Lothian Council before returning to the health service to specialise in health service planning and policy.

In 1985, President Milton Obote invited David to Uganda as a government advisor on health. David met with his then MSP, who introduced him to the Scottish parliament team. With their assistance, David could bring five civil servants to Uganda to implement a government health strategy. To prepare for his trip, David underwent a five-day induction period at parliament.

return to Uganda when his course was done, but a complication had arisen. Uganda had changed its systems that year and stopped hiring male nurses, so he could not use the qualifications he had spent much money on. He returned to school, this time training in National Health Service management.

David met his wife in Glasgow at the Glasgow Royal Maternity Hospital, where she was working as a nurse and neonatal midwife. They married on May 30th, 1981, and settled in Linlithgow, where they lived together until she passed away on May 10th, 2019 (MHSRIP.) David has two sons who live in Uganda.

Although David came with qualifications, having them accredited and recognised in the healthcare system took him a long time. This mirrors the challenges faced by other newcomers. Reflecting on his experience, David says that the road to accreditation might have been even more daunting if he had not been a nurse. David persevered through obstacles and now helps others who are going through similar experiences. He has seen doctors who could not practice because of unrecognised qualifications, encouraging them to persevere and look beyond the immediate obstacles.

After undergoing a lengthy and challenging process of paperwork and bureaucracy, David was finally overjoyed to become a British citizen. His achievement was a powerful symbol of overcoming a system that once felt foreign and out of reach.

David's story goes beyond personal success. He advises others never to lose hope and remain persistent, whether

His father was a local government chief, and his salary was fifteen shillings, which was a lot of money. He has a memory of money being tied to the value of gold. His grandmother was a savvy businesswoman who possessed excellent counting skills. In 1862, when the British arrived in Uganda, she seamlessly transitioned from using cowrie shells to coins. His family comes from Lira District, part of the Lango ethnic group. The Langi people originated from Ethiopia's Abyssinia region and belong to the Nilo-Hamites. Their language is a more straightforward Nilotic tongue that is believed to have become diluted as they migrated southward to their current location between 1800 and 1890.

David, already a qualified medical assistant with two years of work experience at the Gulu Regional Hospital in Uganda, moved to the UK. The forex exchange rate was one-to-one, which meant that the value of Ugandan shillings was equal to that of British pounds. However, a few years after he arrived in the UK, British money underwent a facelift. David recalls an incident where a lady in Newington refused to accept the new two-shilling notes and insisted on receiving her coin back instead.

While on a trip to Manchester, David encountered the differences in currency between regions in the UK for the first time. When he tried to pay for a meal at a restaurant, the waiter refused to accept his Scottish money. David joked and thanked them for the free lunch because he had already finished eating and had no English notes on him. The waiter reluctantly accepted the money after that.

He had come to the UK to pursue further studies. Unfortunately, when he got here, he had to retrain and do general and then psychiatric nursing. He intended to

David Going the Mile - Mafuta Minji

David's childhood memories are filled with shillings and cents, emphasising, "Back when I was a child, money wasn't just about spending—it was about community." He remembers the perception of money or wealth being based on looks. So, a bigger man with a port belly, for instance, was likely to be assumed to be the one with the most money and would often be referred to as "Mafuta Minji", a Swahili word directly translated to mean "A lot of oil" The British drilled holes in the coins they introduced in Uganda because they believed Ugandans couldn't count or lacked pockets for the money. Previously, Uganda, Kenya, and Tanzania shared the East African currency.

investments across different asset classes (stocks, bonds, real estate, etc).

5. Educate Yourself: Invest time in learning about each type of investment you're interested in. Use resources like books, online courses, podcasts, and financial news to build your knowledge.

6. Regularly Review and Adjust: Your financial situation and goals will change, and so will your investment strategy. Regularly review your investments to ensure they align with your current financial goals and risk tolerance.

7. Consider the Long-Term Investing: Investing in the long term is usually the most effective strategy. Despite short-term volatility, the stock market grows over time.

8. Ethical and Socially Responsible Investing: Consider investments that offer financial returns and align with your values. This could mean companies known for being environmentally friendly, socially just, or ethically responsible.

9. Crowdfunding Platforms: Take part in crowdfunding platforms supporting minority-owned businesses or projects with social impact goals. These platforms can offer a way to invest small amounts in causes or businesses you believe in, with the potential for financial returns.

10. Exchange-Traded Funds (ETFs):

These funds are like baskets of stocks or bonds, allowing you to diversify your investments with a single purchase.

2. Start Small but Start Somewhere

You don't need a lot of money to invest. With modern technology and financial products, starting with small amounts is now possible and smart. Here are some accessible investment avenues:

A.) Stock Market: **Fractional Shares allow** you to buy a portion of a stock instead of the whole share, making investing in high-value stocks with less money easier.

- **Exchange-Traded Funds (ETFs):** These funds are like baskets of stocks or bonds, allowing you to diversify your investments with a single purchase.

B.) Peer-to-Peer Lending: Some platforms allow you to lend money directly to individuals or small businesses, earning interest on the loans you give. This can be a more hands-on way to invest and see your money at work.

C.) Online Real Estate Platforms: Some companies allow you to invest in large-scale real estate projects with relatively small amounts of money, offering a way into the property market without the need to buy a whole property.

D.) Cryptocurrency: This is still volatile, but small-scale investments in cryptocurrency can be exciting and put you in with the future of money. Always do thorough research and invest only what you can afford to lose.

3. Automated Investments: Some online services automate investing based on your risk tolerance and goals, making investing easy with little experience.

4. The Importance of Diversification: It's not wise to rely on just one thing for success. To mitigate risk, spread your

Learning Moment: Investing

Eva's top tip: "The key that opens your door in Ghana will not open your door in Scotland." Be humble and open-minded to explore new ways.

Newcomers face unique investment challenges on an uneven playing field. Here's a guide to creating lasting wealth.

Understanding the Landscape

The first step to successful investing is understanding your unique financial landscape. Currency differences, remittance responsibilities, and potential biases in lending practices may affect your investment strategies and outcomes.

A simple and effective strategy, like the 70-10-10-10 principle, can help simplify financial management and establish a strong foundation for growth and stability.

This principle involves allocating 70% of your income towards expenses, 10% towards savings, 10% towards investments, and the remaining 10% towards charitable giving.

Here is some practical information for beginners on investing, focusing on making impactful and unconventional choices.

1. Understanding the Investment Allocation (10%)

First, Investment is using your money to purchase assets that you expect to gain an increase in the original sum invested.

highest wages. Eva brought in the most money when they did a business audit but got the least salary.

Despite this, apart from a Jewish colleague, Eva had more to show in assets and lifestyle than anyone pocketing the bigger paychecks at work.

A Christian preacher, Margaret Wanjiru, who challenged Christians to trust in God instead of buying items on hire purchase, influenced Eva. She always remembered that message and always bought everything in cash.

Eva has dedicated her life to service and community improvement. She created "Healthy Fathering" to encourage fathers' involvement in improving children's futures. Through the Men's Health Forum, she took on the challenges men face, including prejudice and legal obstacles.

Many organisations valued her work because she brought a fresh and unbiased perspective as a woman. She's an inspirational anchor for the African community in Scotland.

asked her to. Feeling mortified and embarrassed, she decided never to lie again and continued her search for a home. Eventually, through divine intervention and sheer determination, Eva purchased her first home. This laid the foundation for a stable future for her and her children. Another smart move she made was that when she got the mortgage, the monthly payments were significantly lower than her rent. Still, Eva continued to pay the same amount, essentially overpaying the mortgage. This enabled her to settle the mortgage on the house sooner.

Eva built up considerable equity after only a few years of owning her home. She invested in a second property and handled the management herself. Unfortunately, this was a mistake, as she ended up with a tenant engaging in illegal activities within the flat. The experience taught a valuable lesson on the necessity of expert advice.

Another difference is that Eva had never heard of child benefits in Ghana, but they became crucial to her financial journey when she moved to Scotland. Instead of seeing this help as a form of charity or windfall of money, Eva viewed it as an investment in her children's future—a seed that would grow into a powerful source of savings and security. So, she never spent it; instead, she opened a separate interest-bearing account where she would keep this money.

She continued to work through upskilling herself and growing her investments despite all the surrounding challenges, including the fact that her employers were racist and her workplace fraught with racial pay gaps where Africans were paid the least, other white people were paid the second least, and the Scottish received the she also started selling Tupperware as Avon sales started dipping.

After her husband decided to pursue his PhD at Strathclyde University, they relocated to Scotland to return to Ghana once he had completed his studies. However, they soon faced unforeseen challenges and curve balls in their new life. One of the main issues was the difficulty that black people, particularly black men like her husband, faced in Scotland.

Then, her husband announced to her he didn't love her any more and wanted a divorce. This was a tough pill to swallow as she had done nothing wrong, and neither had he, but he just declared he had fallen out of love with her; she had five children and was deeply embarrassed and lost. The dissolution of her marriage forced Eva to make a hard choice: succumb to despair or rise with dignity as a single mother of five. She faced a tough period, but her unshakable spirit and Christian faith helped her overcome it and strive for financial independence.

Eva's UK investment journey began with the wave of structural changes started by Margaret Thatcher's new government. These changes included the introduction of privatisation and granting council tenants the right to buy homes. Despite being a single mother of five, Eva felt inspired to explore the possibilities of home ownership. Initially, she approached a mainstream bank but later switched to a building society to secure a mortgage. Navigating the complexities of the Scottish housing market was challenging, but Eva persevered. She recalls an embarrassing incident with a bank manager who asked her what she did for a living. She told him she was a pharmacy assistant but couldn't spell the word pharmacy when he binds the family, but the wife doesn't belong to his bloodline. The husband doesn't leave an inheritance for his children; it defaults to his sister's offspring. The wife's inheritance will go to her children, so women tend to be industrious.

The man raises and provides for the children and even names them, but they ultimately belong to the woman. It is against this backdrop that one of Ghana's educators,

Dr Kwegyir Aggrey said, "If you educate a man, you educate an individual, but if you educate a woman, you educate a nation."

Eva received a little red Bible, which she loved and read. Then she read something that stopped her in her tracks. It said God loves you so much that he has even numbered the very hairs on your head. And she thought, " Oh wow, if this is how my God loves me, then I'm gonna serve him."

So, she started attending the Scripture Union. After high school, Eva went to a teacher training college, where she set up weekly scripture union meetings. During that time, she was proposed to and got married. Soon after the wedding, her husband came to England to do a master's degree. And the church he attended paid for Eva to come and join him. So, in November 1975, Eva relocated to the UK. They were staying in student accommodation, so she made many friends. She also became friendly with a family who adopted her, taking her under their wing. They taught her to bake, knit, & crotchet. Eva learned about Avon and liked the model because it would get her into people's homes and allow her to immerse herself in the culture.

Avon was profitable, and it helped her build relationships, but when affordable makeup became available in stores,

Eva: Strength of a Woman

Aw fur coat, nae knickers!

Well, not Eva Asante; in fact, she's Aw Fur and big, plush knickers!

Eva, an Ashanti royal from Ghana, was raised in a loving home, moving to live with her grandmother when she was five. Eva attended an excellent Methodist church school and learned to carry herself elegantly, speak eloquently, and eat healthily in school. They also learned world history, geography, and many other fascinating things.

In her Ghanaian culture, marriage is matriarchal, with a different concept. Husband and wife have a covenant that

Education and Childcare Strategies: Support your child's learning using free online educational platforms like Khan Academy or BBC Bitesize. Libraries also offer free access to books, educational materials, and activities during school holidays.

Childcare Sharing: Consider forming a childcare co-op with other parents. You can share the responsibility of looking after the children, so you won't have to spend money on childcare. Trust and mutual benefit are key to this arrangement, offering social and financial advantages for all involved.

Healthy Start Vouchers: If you're pregnant or have a child under 4 and you're receiving support from charities or community groups, ask about Healthy Start Vouchers. Although initially intended for those on benefits, organisations may help obtain vouchers for milk, fruits, vegetables, and vitamins.

Use Free Entertainment and Activities: The UK provides plenty of free or low-cost entertainment options for families, such as museums, parks, and community workshops. Check local council websites and community boards for upcoming events.

Energy Saving Measures: Reducing your utility bills can free up a significant amount of money. Use energy-saving bulbs to lower power bills, make free improvements, and find cheaper utility tariffs.

Healthcare and Well-being

The UK's National Health Service (NHS) provides free healthcare for all, including children. However, there may be extra health expenses like dental care (free for kids under 18), glasses, or treatments not covered by the NHS.

Tip: Many employers offer healthcare plans as part of their benefits package, which can cover some of these additional costs. Check if your employer offers any.

Government Support and Benefits

The UK offers various benefits to help families, such as child benefits, which are payments to parents or guardians of children under 16 (or under 20 if in education or training). The eligibility for these benefits can depend on your immigration status and employment situation. To find out which benefits you qualify for and how to apply, visit the UK government's official website or ask a local Citizens Advice Bureau for help.

Leveraging Community and Cultural Networks

Community Support Systems: Tap into the support systems within your cultural or local community. In some communities, families support each other by sharing things like childcare, clothes, and toys in informal groups.

Cultural Associations: Joining a cultural association can provide access to a network that offers financial help, childcare support, interest-free loans, and scholarship opportunities for children's education, creating a sense of belonging.

Learning Moment: Financial Strategies for Raising a Child

Raising a child in the UK can be financially challenging. Planning for expenses related to children can be overwhelming, considering daily expenses and significant costs such as childcare and University tuition fees. To begin with, it is important to create a detailed budget that includes all these expenses and considers the cost of living in your area, which can vary significantly. It is worse if you are navigating the financial landscape of raising a family in the UK without access to public funds.

With creativity, resourcefulness, and the right knowledge, alternative solutions can ease the financial burden. Here are some practical hacks that may help.

Childcare Costs

Childcare expenses are the biggest concern for families, especially those wanting to return to the workforce. Meticulous planning will help, and you should consider all the free or subsidised options available.

The UK government offers free childcare from age three; prior planning for the first two years is vital.

School Expenses

While education is free in the UK, parents should consider extra expenses, such as uniforms, school trips, and activities. If you prefer private education, please remember to budget for fees and typically expensive extracurricular activities.

Start early with tax-beneficial plans like the Junior ISA to save for your child's future education costs.

former dictator president. For Mariama, she thought she was going home done and drained with the UK. She had three children at the time and relocated with them. Well, a complex situation arose because her children were all born and raised in Scotland and then wanted to come back home because home to them was Scotland. An unhappy void Mariama finally feels at home, the kids feeling plucked from home. After long-winded negotiations, it was clear that the intergenerational and multi-cultural conflicts were too many. Identity for Mariama was an immigrant to Scotland, settling back home in the Gambia for her children. They were Scottish first migrating to Gambia. In one conversation, Mariama's daughter said, "Mummy, you are Gambian, and this is your home, but Scotland is ours."

She tried negotiating to bring them to Scotland on holidays, but that didn't work. The children wanted to go Home, and Home to them was Scotland. So back they came! And they came back to nothing because Mariama had gotten rid of everything before they left, plus they were now homeless.

She felt trapped, not wanting to be here, but she was forced to stay here because she'd had children. As a migrant, you uproot yourself from where you are and what you know to plant yourself somewhere new. In Mariama's case, Scotland, that uproot means your roots are unstable. You are still very much back home, but then you have these branches that only know the new reality, so their roots are in the new locale. That is where identity becomes crucial to thriving.

Childcare was a major issue, as there was no family or social capital, and nannies were expensive, leading to a lot of stress.

Interviewer: "Have you worked before?
Mariama: "Yes, I have"
Interviewer: "Can you provide evidence of that?
Mariam: "I would love to, but the company is in Gambia, and the boss was my mum."
Interviewer: "We will be in touch."

She never received a response, and this conversation was repeated at several other interviews. Months later, by some grace, Mariama's aunt, who was working at a hotel as a housekeeper, spoke to her supervisor and got her a job as a cleaner.

The next challenge to navigate became Proof of address because technically, Mariama was at college in London, then travelled to lounge with her brother in Watford for food and most other things and then stayed with her aunt on working days with no bills or any such thing in her name. So, everything seemed to stop without this proof of address because the employer wanted an account to pay the wage into; the bank required this proof of address to give her an account, but the proof of address was impossible to provide with her circumstances and on and on the cycle went.

Eventually and unwillingly prematurely, she had to get her place, raising a whole new raft of challenges.

As time passed, Mariama settled in, had a family, and lived a life with many ups and downs. In 2019, she returned to Gambia. She needed a change in her life and wanted to be closer to her ageing parents after a long, rough ride. She returned to work for the Truth Reconciliation and Reparations Commission in the Gambia, where she investigated human rights violations by the country's

Amiina reconnected with her niece Mariama, who also lived in the UK. Mariama told her that the cost of living was lower in Scotland, and she could find affordable rent. Following Mariama's advice, Amiina moved to Scotland. After she moved, everything changed for the better; she could afford her rent, and her lifestyle improved significantly.

Mariama Jobarteh, is proud of her Gambian heritage. They belong to one of the Griot families, also known as jeliw in some cultures. People respect Griots as narrators of oral traditions. They are also music, poetry, history, genealogy, and storytelling experts. Mariama is from the Mandinka tribe, which has a reputation for drumming and its unique musical instrument, the kora.

Mariama depended on her parents, living, and relying on them until she turned eighteen and was sent to pursue her higher education in the UK. Growing up, money was not a struggle. Her mom owned a Tele centre business, like a centralised phone booth, where people paid to make calls based on how long they spoke and where they were calling. Mariama helped her mom as a cashier for the business, so she got used to handling money, although she would get all the money and pass it on to her mom, who would sort everything else. Before coming to the UK, she had never encountered banks. It was the shock of her life. Mariama remembers coming as a student; her visa had restrictions, but she was allowed to work a few hours. The first huddle was her CV; she needed work experience, but for her, the work experience was in Gambia. Mariama's first interview went downhill after being asked for evidence of her work experience.

So, your parents giving you away to somebody else didn't mean that they didn't love you. Often, they love you and believe you'll have a better life with someone else. You would see them again, and they would continue to be a part of your life, and you would keep visiting, but then you would be under the care of the co-parent you had been given. In Amiina's case, this was her grandma.

They assigned Amiina to her grandmother, after whom she was named. Grandma was a businesswoman from a wealthy family of sugar traders. As Amiina grew older, she realised she was getting spoiled at her grandmother's.

Amiina requested to stay with her dad because she wanted to make something of her life. Her dad was a strict disciplinarian and a high achiever in his own right. Amiina was confident that she had made a good decision for her future. She attended GTTI - Gambia Technical Training Institute for a few years before she got married at 18 because her step-aunts mistreated her.

Amiina married into such a big family that they went through 50 kilograms of rice every week to feed everyone. As a housewife, she managed all the household duties and responsibilities. After a few years of marriage, her husband moved to the UK, and he brought her with him. Amiina and her husband went through some difficulties when they first moved to the UK. They faced multiple evictions, but since they wanted to maintain some stability for their child, they decided not to move him from his school. They had to wake up at 4 AM to ensure he reached school on time. This was on top of a lot of other issues that affected Amiina's mental health.

Amiina & Mariama: Smiling Coast of Africa

Amiina Kahjobarteh was born in Brikama, Gambia, on the smiling coast of Africa.

In the culture of her Gambian people, men can marry up to four wives, resulting in a typically large number of children. Occasionally, parents may give their child to a family member or friend who doesn't have kids or is financially well-off, with no official adoption agreement.

- The STAR technique is a helpful way to answer competency-based questions. You frame your response by discussing the Situation, Task, Action, and Result format, where the Acronym STAR comes from.
Remember that entry-level positions may pay less initially, but you can earn more as you gain experience.

Learning Moment: Positioning Yourself for career success

Kamel recognised the highly competitive environment in his field, where many people vie for coveted positions at esteemed institutions. The competition would be fierce, and his chances of finding a job without experience were even slimmer. So, he showcased his skills by volunteering at a respected but slightly lower-ranked institution.

The strategy had two advantages: it was small enough to be recognised for high performance and big enough to provide a meaningful reference. After just a few months at this institution, a job opportunity arose in the department where he was volunteering. Over 200 applications, including Kamel's, were received for the role, and 12 candidates were shortlisted for three roles. Kamel was among the three who received the job.

Top Tip: Consider starting your career in a rural town. You can save on living expenses and develop a broad range of skills to bring back to the city in the future.

In Kamel's case, choosing a rural hospital within a university was a successful balance for starting his career as a doctor.

Mastering Interview Skills
Interviews in the UK may vary from informal chats to formal panel interviews or competency-based assessments.
- Before your interview, research the company to align your responses with their expectations.
- Practice answering common questions like "Tell me about yourself" and "Why do you want this job?" Also, talk about your strengths and weaknesses to get ready.

Unfortunately, during that time, things took a bad turn in Libya, and war broke out, making it impossible for Kamel to return as planned; it would be ten years before Kamel and his family managed to go back to visit.

Kamel has never had to think about money, per se. Yes, money is essential for survival and to appease his kids and family, but ultimately, he is not driven by money. His career choice and path are driven mainly by a family legacy.

After finishing school and entering the job market, Kamel noticed that every employer wanted proof of previous work experience. The first question they typically asked was, "Where have you worked before?" So, Kamel figured he needed to think strategically about how to deal with that issue.

item on top of that. He was today's equivalent of the Facebook marketplace.

Kamel was the ninth of 10 children, all high achievers—his eldest 86-year-old brother is a medical doctor, his second brother is an engineer, his third one is a medical doctor, then a biochemist, two professors, and so forth. So, career-wise, he had two options—medical Doctor or Engineer.

There was no medical school in Libya at the time, so Kamel started in Italy, where he got his first degree, and then came to Dublin and Scotland to further his studies.

When he opened his bank account in Dublin, he had the smoothest experience, opening his account in under ten minutes. After school, he stayed to do his work experience, never intending to stay forever in Scotland.

Although Kamel's dad was a teacher in the city from the mid-1930s until the early 1980s, most people did not work for the government, so they didn't receive a wage per se. Instead, they bartered. Farmers peddled their produce in exchange for whatever they needed, shepherds traded their sheep and so on and so forth. For non-perishable goods, shopkeepers would warden certain groups of families, opening an account entrusted to the oldest person in each family. Throughout the year, the family would take goods from the shop on credit; the shopkeeper would tally the items and prices in a book - each family had their book, and at the end of the year, the shopkeeper would balance the books up, and come up with a value in animals so if a family owed two sheep, they could either pay in sheep or with the equivalent currency value. It wasn't always rounded off, so someone may owe two sheep and 10 chickens, for example. Or owe one and a half sheep, in which case they may choose to share the difference with another family, or, for example, two brothers may share the animals out to tally up.

There was also another important role in the community of an assessor. His role was to scout for barter opportunities. He would go from village to village ahead of the big market day of each town and pitch at a central location. Then, people would tell him what items they intended to sell, especially if they were items that they couldn't bring to the market. Also, those looking to buy items would tell him what they wanted. He would go through several villages and figure out who could barter with whom. So, if A was interested in a Camel and B was after a silver tray, the assessor would facilitate an exchange between them and work out whatever difference was due to the party with the more valuable

Kamel's childhood memories of 1960s Libya are of a time when the local currency was strong and just a quarter could buy an acre of land in the city. During that time, banking was not common, and the only available bank was The Bank of Roma, which came into existence when the Italians invaded Libya. As a result of this history, the locals did not trust banks and only used them for business purposes. Even then, they were used mainly by society's wealthiest elite.

Kamel's dad was a teacher, and to put this in context, rather than have the salaries paid in a bank, every payday, the School Bursar would take out sacks of cash from the safe and hand out the wages. If people had extra money that they wanted to invest, rather than deposit it in a bank that they didn't trust and was closed at weekends, they would invest in tangible things. Access to cash at the weekend was a big deal; Libyans are very social and love entertaining; the thought of having guests - (a common occurrence for friends and family to turn up unannounced) and not being unable to buy and slaughter an animal for a feast quickly was unthinkable. It was better to hold your cash in animals, keep it in a glass jar that would be buried for safekeeping or, for longer-term investing, buy camels or sheep that could soon be converted should you need them.

They would buy camels and sheep and send them outside the city with a hired shepherd if they didn't have enough land. The shepherd would accept sheep from different people so that each person would pay a small percentage of the shepherd's wage and upkeep. The shepherd was a great custodian and kept excellent records of what animals belonged to whom, tallying and marking the animals with different symbols to track them.

sites, built by the Romans. Although Libya had Roman settlers 2000 years ago and then was later colonised by Italy, its national language is Arabic, and most of its population primarily speaks Arabic. Nearly 100% of native Libyans are Muslims. Kamel's father studied in an Italian school and spoke Italian quite fluently, as does Kamel, but what Libya inherited from Italy was not the language. Historically, there were no Libyan schools, so everyone went through the Italian education system. Libya inherited the technical terms of things rather than the Italian language.

Several countries, including Italy, colonised Libya, but the Libyan people never welcomed foreign rule. After years of conflict, Libya gained independence and became a recognised sovereign nation in 1951. Before its independence, the land now known as Libya was a semi-independent province of the Ottoman Empire from 1711 to 1835, an Italian colony from 1912 until 1947, and was under British and French occupation from 1943 to 1951.

The lead-up to independence was intriguing. When the initial United Nations vote was cast, the results were an equal split, with 50% of the delegates voting for and 50% against.

The Libyan representative convinced the Haitian representative, pleading with him to imagine it was his country, Haiti, and whether he would like to be under foreign occupation. It worked; when the vote was recast the next day, Haiti changed its vote and Libya gained independence. Libya was very grateful and named a street after Haiti.

Kamel: Completely Successfully Blessed

Kamel Elnageh's name has an interesting meaning: Kamel stands for Complete, and Elnageh means Success. He comes from the historical city of Sabha, which is situated just 60 kilometres west of Tripoli, the capital city of Libya in North Africa. Sabra and Sabratha are two ancient Roman cities over 2000 years old and are among the best-preserved Roman sites outside Italy. The theatre is still in use today and is one of the world's best archaeological

Get in front of customers: You must focus on getting your product or service in front of customers as soon as possible. While perfecting your offering is critical, talking to your customers, understanding their needs, and making sales to keep your business running are also important. So, aim to get to the market as soon as possible.

Step 7: Navigating Challenges with Resilience

- Prepare for Financial Instability: Side hustles can have inconsistent incomes, especially at the start. Budget wisely and have a financial buffer to manage slow months.

Seek Mentors and Advice as soon as possible: Connect with other entrepreneurs or mentors through platforms like LinkedIn or local business hubs and meetups. Their experience can offer guidance and prevent you from making common mistakes.

Step 4: Simplified Business Planning

- Use Smart Planning Methods: Instead of a traditional business plan, use a one-page business model canvas to visualize your business idea, target market, and value proposition quickly and clearly.

-Set Realistic Goals: It's essential to set clear, achievable short-term goals for your side hustle. These goals could include landing a specific number of customers, hitting a sales target, or launching your business successfully.

Step 5: Building Your Presence and Networking

- Create a low-cost online presence by utilising social media platforms such as Instagram, Facebook, or LinkedIn to create a professional profile for your side hustle. Even if you have yet to gain design experience, tools like Canva can help you design marketing materials.

- Engage with Local Communities Online and Offline: Connect with local communities online and offline. You can join Facebook groups, participate in forums, attend community events, or use platforms dedicated to event meetups and neighbourhood building.

Step 6: The Lean Startup way

- Start Small and Iterate: To minimise your risk and test the market, start with a product or service that is small or cheap but delivers enough value to entice customers to purchase it. This is commonly known as a minimal viable product (MVP). It will allow you to gather feedback from early customers, which is invaluable for refining your offerings.

Step 2: Understand Your Tax Obligations in the UK.

When you start earning additional income, it's important to inform HM Revenue & Customs (HMRC) about it. You can do this by filling out a Self-Assessment tax return, which is the way to report your side hustle earnings. Even if your income is below the tax threshold, informing HMRC will help you keep accurate tax records. Again, it is possible to do this online.

If your side hustle's turnover exceeds the VAT threshold, you must register for VAT. However, even if your turnover is below the threshold, voluntary VAT registration can benefit you by allowing you to reclaim VAT on business expenses.

Step 3: Do your market research and identify a niche.

- Leverage Your Cultural Uniqueness: As a newcomer, your unique cultural background can be an advantage in a competitive market. You can leverage your cultural identity to provide customers with authentic experiences such as traditional cuisine, crafts, storytelling, and language services. Your cultural heritage can set you apart from others in the market.

- Take advantage of free research tools. Insights into trending topics can be gained through Google Trends, social media, and Subreddits related to the UK or specific to sectors you are considering, which can be goldmines of information.

Learning Moment: The Side Hustle is possible; start a business

For newcomers to the UK, achieving financial stability can be a complex task. Many people look for ways to supplement their income while pursuing a new life in the country. This is where the concept of side hustles comes in handy. A side hustle is a secondary job or a small business you can do alongside your primary occupation. Side hustles can provide financial freedom and help you integrate more fully into your new community.

Step 1: Verify Your Legal Standing

- Before you start looking for a job, you must check the restrictions on your visa or immigration status. Certain visas may limit the type of work you are allowed to do or restrict the number of hours you can work outside of your primary Visa purpose. For more information, visit the official website of the UK government.

Register for a **National Insurance Number**: If you plan to work in the UK, you'll need a National Insurance (NI) number. This is necessary for tax purposes and can be applied for through the Department for Work and Pensions (DWP). The UK is now primarily digital, and most of these applications can be made online.

If you don't have access to the Internet, find your local library. They will typically have access to free Wi-Fi and computers that you can use to research and check applications for some of these things.

account to repay it in full by direct debit every month. So, she kept her wise habit of checking affordability before spending. She would still check her bank account to see if she could pay back the total amount at the end of each month.

For the first-generation migrant parent, it is a trifold existence, holding onto old values from a heritage unknown in the new environment through a lens only the migrant can translate, attempting to overlay it with the cherry picks of the new culture in an attempt to create a third reality of a mix of the two cherry picks, hoping for a perfect third alternative. For the child - the second-generation migrant, it's yet a further complexity of a seemingly fully present and immersed cultural experience in their environment overlaid by an acute awareness of the parent's native norms juxtaposed with a layer of a window into another universe, usually more folklore and mythically played out in their daily home life by a parent clinging onto their past, putting them on the fringes of any sphere where they are in but out, knowledgeable but not full partakers of their realities. The banking system was another, haha; they didn't have credit cards in Nigeria, so she hadn't been exposed to them while growing up. So, the concept sounded dodgy when Ife first heard of them. Knowing what she knew, Ife concluded there must be a catch: "no such thing as a free dinner" - she thought. So, she made them a taboo; her bank would send messages telling her she qualified for a credit card, and she would ignore them, preferring to pay cash and full price than to take out any loans or facilities. Then she was told that if she didn't get a credit card, she couldn't be considered creditworthy and that if they ever wanted to buy a house with a mortgage, they would need to be credit-worthy. So, she got a credit card and shoved it inside the furthest drawer, never using it once. Then she heard that that was pointless and that getting the credit card and not using it was as bad as not having one at all. She learned that she had to use it and pay it back to show creditworthiness, so she started using the credit card and set up her bank the British postcards and books painted of picturesque white snowflake specs; the reality was a soggy brown mess a few hours after the snowfall. She couldn't believe a place like this existed. It was miserable, and Ife wanted to return to sunny Nigeria.

Her husband tried to placate her, consoling her that they would make it work, but too distraught to follow, she spent her first months bitterly depressed. She fell pregnant quickly, and it was only when she started preparing for the bundle of joy that she eventually settled in.

Raising Scottish children has also been a journey, a complex multi-dimensional existence - for any migrant.

As Ife completed her secondary school education and proceeded to university, she became more involved in managing her mother's businesses. She transformed one of the businesses into a wholesale distributor of yams and other agricultural produce, which they sold to market vendors. Additionally, Ngo had a second business that produced coconut candy, and Ife took over the operations of that business. Ife would purchase coconut in bulk while stocking up for the wholesale shop and process it into delicious coconut chips, known as Chop One Chop Two in slang. Since Ngo started running the business, a customer base had already been established, making it easy for Ife to keep it going.

Ife and her childhood friend fell in love again after reconnecting. He had moved to Scotland as a student, and they started a long-distance relationship. Eventually, he returned to Nigeria, and they got married. He arranged for Ife to join him in Scotland, but she hesitated to leave her comfortable life in Nigeria with her family and friends. Unfortunately, due to tradition, Ife had to move to her husband's location after the wedding.

Moving to Scotland brought numerous cultural and transitional shocks. She married at 24 and had never lived independently, so she was clueless about running a household. While she was astute with managing her mom's businesses, running a home was too much. She went straight from her parent's house to her husband's, with nothing in between.

It did not help that Ife moved to Scotland during the winter; a few days after she arrived, she was welcomed by a big snowstorm. It was her first snow experience, which was thick, knee-deep, and freezing. So much for all the lies prepared the afternoon meal. The one who went to school in the morning returned home in the afternoon, and the other house helper went to school. This way, one house helper was always home to look after the children and prepare the evening meal.

Ife learned a lot from her mother and grandmother. She remembers her grandmother as kind and angelic. She was the best grandmother anyone could ask for, and Ife is grateful to see her mother being just like her with her children. Ife remembers going to grandma's market stall growing up, and if a child came to buy stuff and had little money, if grandma knew the family was big, she would throw in more things for the whole family. Her stall was a community favourite. This instilled kindness in Ife. She saw first-hand that it's not all about money. Love, compassion, and giving oneself to humanity are worth much more than money.

Ife's eldest sister was named after their maternal grandmother, and she was automatically assigned to her, so she would get to visit grandma most of the time. This irked Ife as she loved being with her grandmother and wished she was the one named after her. During the Christmas holidays, they visited their grandparents, but they were obliged to spend more time with their paternal grandmother; they preferred their maternal grandmother Ngo's mum and would connive and appeal to spend more time with their maternal grandmother. Unfortunately, they had to go to their paternal grandmother's house as traditionally; mom was obliged to default to her husband's family as expected; after a woman wed, she left her parents and defaulted to her husband's family.

Mum made sure that Ngo was always close to her. This allowed Ngo to witness her mother's entrepreneurial lifestyle closely, and she learned much about money and trade. Mum was very frugal and not extravagant, so she was always budgeting. Some of Ngo's brothers were also involved in the business and had to help before going to school every morning, which also taught them time management.

Ngo was married just before she turned 15. During those times, once a girl had started menstruating, she was deemed mature enough to bear children and was married off at any time after her first period. In Ngo's case, her marriage was a practical arrangement instigated by her husband, who expressed interest in her and approached her family for her hand in marriage. Her parents signed on her behalf and made the necessary arrangements with the husband's family.

Ife, Ngo's daughter, had a different experience than her mother. She married for love on her terms and cannot imagine how her mother managed to raise seven children. Ife has three children and often forgets her name in the morning.

During Ngo's time, they had house help and nannies to support raising the children. Ngo had a government job and an evening hustle of food vending, which she inherited from her mother's business. She would be away from home for long hours to ensure she could provide food for her family.

Ngo had two house helpers who were slightly older than her children. They worked on rotation, one attending morning school while the other cleaned the house and

Ife & Ngo: Chop one, Chop two

Ngo and Ife are a mother and daughter from Enugu state in Nigeria. When Ngo was younger, her mom ran a small business that traded as a food vendor, which helped support the family. Ngo was the fourth child of seven and the only girl among them. Ngo's brothers used to try to spoil her, but their mom wouldn't allow it. She would say, "I have only one daughter; I don't want her to be spoiled."

- **Section 17 Support**: Under Section 17 of the Children Act 1989, local authorities have a duty to safeguard and promote the welfare of children in need. This can sometimes provide a basis for families with No Recourse to Public Funds to access accommodation and financial help.

- **Destitution Domestic Violence Concession (DDVC)**: This is available for those on a spousal visa experiencing domestic violence, allowing them to access public funds for a limited period while they apply for indefinite leave to remain under the Domestic Violence Rule.

- **Change of Conditions Application**: If someone's circumstances change, they may apply to the Home Office to have the No Recourse to Public Funds condition lifted from their immigration status, allowing them to access public funds. This is particularly relevant for those who prove denying access to public funds would breach their rights under the Human Rights Act.

4. Faith-Based Organizations: Churches, mosques, temples, and other faith communities often offer support to members of their community, including food, clothing, and sometimes financial assistance or shelter.

Learning Moment: Available Financial Support

If you're new to the UK and seeking financial guidance, several impartial services are designed to assist you in understanding and managing your finances effectively. Here's a non-exhaustive list based on the time of writing. Please check often to ensure that you have the most up-to-date information.

1. Food banks: Are often associated with a negative stigma. Many people wrongly assume that accessing a food bank means you have failed. However, this is not the case. In reality, acknowledging that you need support and taking steps to access that support can prove powerful and useful. So, overlook the negative assumptions and recognise that accessing a food bank is positive. It means you are taking proactive steps to get the help you need.

2. Free Newspapers: Most bus services offer free newspapers you can pick up. You may get valuable information from the newspaper that would be difficult to gather if you rely solely on unguided internet searches. While the internet is great, too much information can also be overwhelming. A newspaper provides limited and categorised information, making it easier to find specific and accurate information that is more relevant to your location.

3. Legal Advice: Various organisations offer free legal advice to immigrants on immigration matters, including potential pathways to regularise their status and access public funds. The Law Centres Network, Citizens Advice, and other legal charities can assist.

classmate was surprised to hear this and decided to visit the food bank based on Justin's recommendation.

Certainly, finding ways to alleviate the mental strain that comes with financial difficulties is important. As an international student, it is crucial to prioritise paying your fees and rent, which is where financial assistance programs like food banks can be helpful. By taking advantage of these programs, you can avoid defaulting on payments, which can cause a lot of mental pressure and lead to losing access to your student portal and school work.

Justin discovered that the University offers support for students who are struggling financially. This includes payment holidays or plans for school fees. In extreme cases, the University can provide support from internal funds that do not breach visa restrictions. It is essential to seek help when needed to avoid the stress and anxiety that financial difficulties can cause.

Justin's determination and adaptability paid off. He completed his Master's degree and is currently gaining work experience in Scotland. His journey from Nigeria to the UK was full of challenges, but he persevered and adapted to the changes with resilience and determination. His experiences highlight the importance of being open-minded, adaptable, and resourceful when navigating new environments. His story highlights the value of education and the power of hard work, perseverance, and excellence. It inspires all those who aspire to pursue their dreams and achieve success despite the odds.

Justin was resourceful in finding solutions to his financial struggles. He discovered a local food bank that helped him manage his food expenses, allowing him to allocate more money to other areas of his life. He even referred his classmates to the food bank, as some were unaware of its existence. He had found out about them through church, which he found to be a great source of information and knowledge.

Justin observed that some of his classmates felt ashamed to use the food bank. He encouraged them to give it a try. Justin told one of his classmates about his experience at the food bank, where he saw people from different backgrounds, including Scots and Asians. He noticed that everyone was treated with respect and dignity. His

calculated based on the number of hours worked. This new system required a major change in behaviour and a new framework of financial discipline and adaptability. Justin had to unlearn everything he knew to adjust to this new way of managing his finances.

His student visa allowed him to work 20 hours a week, which initially seemed like a great opportunity. Yet, when he started working part-time, he realised his pay was insufficient to cover his expenses in the UK and support his young family back home in Nigeria.

Justin realised he needed to prioritise his expenses and couldn't be extravagant. These adjustments were defining moments for Justin, who learned to make quick decisions and understood the importance of caring for one's mental and overall well-being. Nevertheless, Justin was determined to integrate and immerse himself. Continuing with his excellence streak, Justin soon got elected as the student representative at the University. With hundreds of students relying on him for support, staying focused and finding solutions for their problems was important.

The plus side to this was that it helped Justin learn the ropes himself despite going through his issues. For a start, taking on the student representative role came with some training from the university, which was very helpful in knowing what to expect and how to navigate things in the UK. So, while it was a volunteer role, it had many positives. He got to meet many people involved in his local community. If you're a student, volunteering can be a great way to support others and integrate into the community.

students from different universities and formed great friendships.

After Justin graduated from university, he had to complete a compulsory one-year national service - called NYSC (National Youth Service Corps). This is a government initiative to promote unity amongst the over 500 tribes of Nigeria. The idea is to encourage cohesion by exposing people to different cultures and tribes. For example, if you are from Kaduna state in the north, you may be posted to Lagos state in the west. After completing his compulsory service, Justin continued to work at the same commercial bank for about ten years.

Justin decided to enhance his qualifications and started exploring his options for further education. He found the UK to be a great fit for several reasons: 1) A Master's degree from the UK is highly respected in Nigeria; 2) The time difference between the two countries is only one to two hours; 3) The flight time is approximately 4-5 hours. So, he decided to pursue his education in the UK.

That was the easy part of Justin's next phase. Arriving in the UK was a baptism of bitterly cold winter for Justin, a stark contrast to the hot climate of Nigeria. He kicked off his addiction to tea and coffee in pursuit of warmth and quickly cranked up his energy bills.

This challenge was soon followed by the realisation that the UK financial system operated at an entirely different pace. Justin was accustomed to paying for his accommodation in annual rent payments and receiving a fixed monthly salary, regardless of the number of hours he worked. However, he found himself in a new world where rent needed to be paid monthly, and wages were finish their money, that they had so much they couldn't spend it all. It was common for Nigerians to send money abroad to support loved ones studying or living outside the country, thanks to the Palm Oil and the Petroleum oil boom that Nigeria enjoyed for a long while.

The other memorable thing Justin remembers is the tangible reward of academic excellence. Nigerian schools grade students from first to last position based on academic performance. The top three students often receive prizes from the school authorities in a prize-giving ceremony where awards are given, including monetary prizes for top-performing students.

Additionally, organisations may sponsor awards, tuition relief, and other scholarships named after them. These incentives encourage students to excel academically as early as primary school.

Because of this, the attitude to school is that it pays, so the ultimate goal was to achieve the highest possible grade at the highest educational level. The culture is so ingrained that dropping out is typically frowned upon.

Thankfully, Justin was a top performer. On several occasions, he fondly recalls his dad having guests over and calling Justin to bring his report and show it to the guests. Dad would beam with pride and list Justin's accolades that year.

Knowing that his investment in Justin's education was paying off was always a source of pride for his dad.

During his university years, Justin worked part-time over the Christmas and Easter holidays. He enjoyed meeting

Justin: Hard Work Pays

Justin grew up in Nigeria and fondly recalls living in a close-knit neighbourhood where everyone knew everyone and the children belonged to the neighbourhood.

If a child misbehaved, any adult had an

equal right to discipline them as if they were their own. Creating a deep sense of community and family, people referred to each other as brothers and sisters regardless of biological relation and meant it. So, sharing was the way of life, thriving on mutual respect, support, and a deep-seated tradition of sharing, be it food, joy, or the burdens of life.

During that time - between the 1970s and 1980s, Nigeria was economically strong. In fact, the Naira was stronger than the US dollar, and the pound was only one to two Naira. There was such a flow of wealth that there was a long-standing joke about Nigerians not knowing how to

2. Cultural and Community Centers: Many cultural and community centres in the UK organise groups and activities, including Money Clubs, to help newcomers integrate and find support. Visiting these centres can connect you with a Money Club that aligns with your background and financial goals.

Starting your Own: If you can't find a Money Club that suits you, consider starting your own. Use social media or community notice boards to express your interest and connect with others in a similar situation. Starting with people with similar circumstances can establish a strong foundation of mutual understanding and support.

Joining a Money Club can help your financial growth; it's more than finding a community and support in a new environment. It's a way to learn about managing finances in the UK, share experiences, and build connections beyond money. Approach with patience, caution, and openness, and you'll find that Money Clubs can offer much more than financial benefits—they can offer a sense of belonging.

2. Clear Rules and Structure: A well-organised Money Club should have clear rules about contributions, distributions, and what happens if someone fails. Before joining, please ensure you have a written agreement or a clear understanding of all terms.

3. Transparency: Choose a club that maintains transparent and precise records of all transactions and meetings. Open communication about the club's finances should be accessible to all members. If the club uses technology to improve the safety of making and receiving contributions, ask why they don't if they don't use any technology.

4. Legal Review: Even though Money Clubs are informal, it's important to ensure they operate within the legal frameworks of the UK, especially concerning money handling and taxes.

5. Cultural and Language Compatibility: For newcomers, finding a club that shares your cultural background or language can make the experience more comfortable and enriching.

How to Find a Money Club

1. Online Communities and Forums: Research online platforms like Meetup, Facebook groups, or community forums specific to your nationality or interests in the UK. These spaces often post about existing Money Clubs looking for new members or others interested in starting one. If you are a student, check with your student union to see if there are any Money Clubs on campus.

help you and your friends achieve your goals faster than you would.

Benefits of Participating in a Money Club

Savings Discipline: By making regular contributions to a money club, you can develop a disciplined approach to saving money.

Access to Lump Sums: Money clubs operate rotationally, meaning each member receives a lump sum when their turn comes up. This lump sum can be useful for meaningful purchases or investments. For example, Shupikai used her lump sum to buy a car, which helped to kickstart her taxi side business.

Nurturing Relationships: A Money Club fosters community and mutual support among its members. As all members are part of something shared, Money Clubs tend to nurture relationships.

What to Consider

It is important to note that putting your money into a Money Club is not protected by the Financial Services Compensation Scheme (FSCS). If the scheme goes bankrupt or your money is lost, you cannot get it back. If this is a significant concern for you, one regulated option you can consider is Credit unions, which are protected under FSCS. These are member-run organisations where members pool their savings to lend to one another.

1. Trust and Security: Trust is the foundation of a Money Club. You can take the time to get to know potential group members before you start contributing money. It's best to start with smaller amounts until you feel confident that the group is trustworthy.

Learning Moment: Leveraging Money Clubs

Moving to the UK can be exciting but poses specific challenges, particularly when managing money in a new country. One way to navigate these challenges while building a support network could be by joining a Money Club.

If you're new to the UK and want to know how to get started, this beginner-friendly guide will help you find your community and make wise financial decisions together.

What is a Money Club?

A money club, also known as a Rotating Savings and Credit Association (ROSCA), is an informal financial group that has existed for centuries across various cultures worldwide. In the UK, ROSCAs are common among immigrant communities and groups of people who often have limited access to traditional banking services.

Money Clubs provide financial and social support based on mutual trust and shared goals. In a money club, a group of people agree to contribute a fixed amount to a central pot at regular intervals. The total amount collected at each interval is given to one member on rotation until all members have received the pot.

Joining a Money Club can be an effective and enjoyable way to reach your financial objectives. The concept is that in every cycle (typically monthly), each member contributes a set amount of money to a group pot. One member receives the entire sum each month, which they can use to accomplish a substantial goal, such as repairing a car, paying for a course, or even starting a small business. This collaborative approach to saving money can

Shupikai was determined to maintain her African culture even after coming to Britain. Her experience in Britain helped her appreciate her identity on a deeper level. Therefore, when she had her children, she made it a point to speak to them in her mother tongue. She did this so that when they visit Zimbabwe and Botswana, they can connect with their roots and family there. As there is already a geographical boundary between her children and their roots, teaching them her local dialect helps keep them rooted in their culture. Shupikai's Christian faith has been an anchor for her, helping her navigate her life wisely as a Scottish Zimbabwean.

Despite Shupikai's initial hesitation, her aunt's unwavering belief and insistence that she give the UK a chance were too persistent to ignore. "Take a chance," her aunt urged her as she presented Shupikai with an opportunity to switch from a visitor's visa to a working visa. During the visit to her aunt's place, her aunt offered her a job on the condition that she convert her visa to a work permit. After much persuasion, Shupikai decided to stay and study while working part-time for her aunt. A few years later, she visited her sister in Scotland, and her husband mentioned that a friend was looking for a driver. Even though she already had a job, Shupikai loved the pace and nature of Scotland and decided to take the job. The job came with a car, a house, and everything Shupikai needed to settle in Scotland. She was given a week-long orientation by one of the staff members, and after that, she was left to manage herself.

Adjusting to life in the UK was another ball game, very different from her move from Zimbabwe to Botswana. The lifestyle, the people, and the politics were all different. On paper, it seemed like she was earning more money, but it didn't go as far as it had in Botswana. In addition, there was the challenge of understanding the cultural norms, legal rights, and dos and don'ts; everything was just unfamiliar. Shupikai faced many challenges but was determined to regain her status in Botswana. She persevered through all the hardships and learned to fight. However, there came a point when she had to keep going because the life she knew before and the people at that time had moved on. So, she had to double down and make Scotland her new home. Once she took that leap of faith, there was no turning back.

She quickly became successful in Botswana as an assistant hotel manager, making friends and settling into her new life. Meanwhile, Shupikai maintained her connections in Zimbabwe and continued to be part of her long-standing "Mukando" group. This was a round-table savings club where she and a group of women pooled together to save a set amount of money each month. They took turns receiving a lump sum to spend as they pleased. When it was Shupikai's turn to receive the Mukando money, she bought a taxi and hired a driver to start her taxi business side hustle. Her hard work and dedication paid off when her manager heard about her new business. She was on good terms with her manager, who gave her a contract to transport hotel guests and staff, and she jumped at the opportunity. Her manager became her first loyal corporate client, hiring Shupikai's taxi for hotel guests and staff in exchange for a retainer fee, and the "pula", Botswana's currency, which means "rain" in Setswana, continued to shower Shupikai. She accumulated more money, and when her next Mukanda came, she bought two more taxis.

Shupikai's life took an unexpected turn during a visit from her aunt, who lived in the UK. Her aunt invited her to see her in the UK. Although Shupikai initially hesitated to leave her businesses and the life she had built in Botswana behind, she reluctantly decided to visit the UK on a short holiday.

Looking back at her journey, Shupikai shares that she never dreamed of her current situation. However, destiny had other plans for her, and by accepting her aunt's invitation, her life took a different course, leading her from Zimbabwe to Botswana and ultimately to Britain.

senior police officer in their community, became an excellent role model for her. He was an accomplished man, devoted to his family and admired by all who knew him for his guidance and inspiration.

Living with her brother was an incredible experience for Shupikai, and it was during this time that she had some of the most memorable moments of her life. Even after her brother's death, he remains Shupikai's most inspirational role model. Her greatest comfort is that the police department recognised how special he was and gave him a dignified state funeral with a well-deserved gun salute.

After graduating from high school, she decided to pursue her lifelong dream of a career in hotel management. So, with her brother's help, she enrolled in college and dedicated herself to her studies, always eager to learn and improve her skills. She did very well in her course, and after graduating, she got a job at a prestigious hotel in Bulawayo. Shupikai was a natural at hotel management, and her diligent work ethic quickly earned her a reputation as a competent and dedicated employee. Her colleagues and superiors respected and admired her, and her career took off due to her hard work and determination.

After a while, Shupikai was offered an excellent opportunity to move to Botswana to work in a more prestigious hotel. At the time, Zimbabwe was experiencing financial difficulties, making life difficult for its citizens. However, Botswana was flourishing, with a surge in diamond revenue and an influx of tourists visiting the vast Kalahari Desert and lush Okavango Delta. So, choosing to relocate was easy.

Shupikai: A tale of three currencies

Shupikai spent her early years in the bustling city of Bulawayo, the second-largest city in Zimbabwe. Sadly, her mother died when she was just three years old, and her loving grandmother raised her. Despite the tragedy of losing her mother, Shupikai's childhood was filled with happiness and simplicity. She was surrounded by a large, caring family who showered her with love and affection, and she never experienced lack or sadness. She spent most of her days playing outside and enjoying the beauty of nature. When Shupikai started primary school, she moved in with her father and lived with him until she finished high school. However, after her father remarried, she found safety and protection in the care of her older brother. Her brother, who happened to be a respected

Use such cards cautiously for routine purchases and ensure they're paid off in full monthly.

Leverage International Presence

If you have banked with global institutions, there's a silver lining. Some international Banks offer the possibility of transferring your banking history, easing your way into the UK's financial system. This continuity can be beneficial for opening new accounts and getting credit without the usual newcomer hurdles. Check if your Bank is international.

Credit Unions

Do consider joining a credit union. They often provide more personalised financial products with better rates than traditional banks. Credit unions can also accommodate those without a UK credit history, offering a more flexible approach to lending and banking.

The financial landscape in the UK is ever-changing, with new products and promotions continually emerging. You can make it a habit to review your banking arrangements often. Switching accounts or services could unlock better deals and even earn you cashback on switching offers that will enhance your financial well-being.

Learning Moment: Navigating the UK Banking System

Understanding the banking system is your first step towards long-term prosperity in a new country.

Opening a bank account, typically a current account for daily transactions and a savings account for earning interest on your reserved money. Identification and proof of address are essential for account setup, which is traditionally a minimum requirement.

Understanding the concept of a credit score is critical, as it influences your ability to borrow money or secure credit cards; building a good credit history through responsible financial behaviour is vital. The UK offers solid online banking services that could save you time and help you get up to speed quicker. For international money transfers, consider using specialised services for better rates. Familiarise yourself with the safety nets provided, such as the Financial Services Compensation Scheme that protects your savings deposits up to £85,000 as of this moment (This gets revised depending on the economy, so always bear that in mind.

Building a Strong Foundation: The Power of Credit

Creating a robust credit history in the UK might seem daunting, but it's a key part of your financial Identity. Start by exploring banking relationships that favour the growth of your credit score. Opening both a savings and a current account with the same bank improves your standing with that bank. There are also products like credit builder credit cards specifically designed for people aiming to establish a solid credit footprint.

her mother in memory of a time when she sacrificed everything, walking barefoot so her children would go to school.

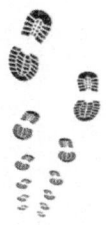

presents and wrap them up as if they had come from their different aunts and grandparents from Kenya so that they had loads under the tree and they didn't feel less than or left out when their peers at school were constantly showered with gifts and money from grandparents and relatives. So that at least they could also go to school and say, "I got this from my aunt or gran." Mukami took her children to Kenya every year at considerable expense, which she couldn't afford, but it was a better investment than buying a Gucci handbag.

She found the UK banking system oppressive and horrible to people like her, riddled with exorbitant money transfer fees and high interest rates for services. She remembers arguing with her bank manager because she had taken a bridging loan and was charged much higher than the advertised rates. Mukami once heard someone saying that if you owe the bank thousands of pounds, they invite you for breakfast to discuss the terms with you, but if you owe them hundreds, they send you the bailiffs. She has found institutions to be hostile to Africans: "Our values are only useful when they're being exploited". It is shameful that, till today, most African currencies are pegged to the dollar.

Mukami is now a Chocho—grandmother, among many other notable accolades. She has had an impressive career and impact on Scotland, influencing and driving policy change for 30 years, promoting Gender Equality and Women's rights. She is the current chair and founder of KWISA (Kenyan Women in Scotland Association), a board member for Christian Aid, and was awarded an MBE for her work and campaign for human rights.

She has participated in massive fundraising campaigns and is most proud of the 1,000 shoes project she dedicated to

Mukami also soon realised that her colleagues didn't have the qualifications she had. Her managers barely had as high an education. She experienced firsthand how people get trapped in jobs for which they are overqualified.

Mukami lost her professional right to teach in school, a significant loss. Being a teacher in Kenya was prestigious, especially as a young black professional, when Europeans and Asians occupied most of the professional jobs. Coming to Scotland, even getting a supermarket checkout job was almost impossible. She had to reinvent many aspects of her Identity. In Kenya, she was part of the Majority. Suddenly, coming here, she was classed as a Minority. Then there was the Identity as Afro-Caribbean, and again, she wasn't comfortable with this - She felt entirely African and not part Caribbean, yet here they were being bundled together.

As she settled in, Mukami noticed that British people seemed flippant with money. She recalls a scenario when she had progressed in her career, being a CEO, and her admin officer laughing at her because she drove an old car. But Mukami preferred to buy a second-hand car because the difference was money she could send back home. Her colleagues seemed to spend money on the airiest things spontaneously. She marvelled at how easy money seemed for them and how useless it was simultaneously. She understood in these moments how easily one's mental health can deteriorate if one continues comparing one's home country with being abroad, especially if you're not earning enough to meet costs in both countries.

It was a challenging journey for Mukami. She recalls how dreary Christmas could be because she didn't have her family surrounding her. She would buy her children

When a Kikuyu woman gets married, she leaves her home and people to set roots among her husband's people. So, when Mukami married a Scot, the Scottish people became her people, and Scotland became her country.

Mukami came to Scotland in 1973 with her Scottish husband from Kenya. At 75 years old, she has lived in Scotland longer than in Kenya. She arrived with her husband (MHSRIP), intending to visit for only one year. They had met as teachers, both working in a Kenyan school. They have two children, one born in Kenya and the other in Scotland. As the children got older, relocating became more difficult because they could only leave when not in school. So, they stayed in Scotland because of circumstances rather than a plan.

That 8-hour flight from Nairobi to London and then Scotland, intended as a one-year visit, completely changed Mukami's life and identity. First, she couldn't work in Scotland because she was not GTC registered, a legal requirement for Qualified Teacher Status in schools. Despite being educated in the British system with Overseas Cambridge University qualifications, Mukami was told she would have to go back to retrain for three years to become a teacher in Scotland.

Moreover, with young children and having left all semblance of family as she knew it back in Kenya, she struggled with childcare and gave up on her teaching career. However, she was keen to work and finally found a job at a supermarket looking after plants. To her surprise, Mukami earned more as a supermarket plant assistant than in her prestigious teaching position in Kenya.

was given the same patch she had dug up the year before. She dug, and she dug, but there wasn't a sign of any sweet potato in her patch; she couldn't believe that everyone else seemed to have so many sweet potatoes. Getting frustrated, she grumbled and sulked, asking her peers, "Why have you given me this barren patch? There's not a root of a potato in here." The other woman turned and said, "Remember what you did last year? You pulled out every bit of sweet potato harvesting, even the tiniest roots, which were supposed to grow for the next season; now you have nothing." Likewise, with food, greed was frowned upon. Mukami was taught never to take more food than others. Food may be served buffet-style, but the unspoken expectation was that wherever you were in the queue, you needed to look around and assess how big the queue was to determine how much to serve yourself. The culture was Harambee:

All Pull Together & Ubuntu: Humanity to Others.

because they would be travelling through the big town, where it was likely that money in your pocket may get stolen, so sewing it into their clothing ensured they didn't lose their school fees.

Mukami's father worked in the White Highlands, and they lived in the native reserves. During the holidays, they would travel to the White Highlands, and that's when Mukami found out that her mother used to sew money into their clothes because she would say, "Don't put those clothes in water."

Aside from that, going to high school, for example, they didn't get pocket money, or it wasn't something you thought about. Sometimes, when people came from the city to visit them in the rural areas, they would give them coins, which they would hand to their mother. And sometimes, their mother went to the market and brought them sweets, which again was a rare one-off.

But they learned about conservation, saving, and other practical manners. For example, they grew maize in their garden and were trained never to eat the best maize. Their mother would select the best maize cob to be kept for planting next season. The lesson was that they must keep the best for the future, and it was instilled in them.

They were told a folk tale of a woman who came to visit her friend, and they went out to the garden to harvest sweet potatoes in a patch. The guest dug out everything in the patch she was given, including the tiny little roots. At the end of the harvest day, she had a big sack and went home with the most sweet potatoes. The other women had enough sweet potatoes to last them through that season. The following year, the woman visited again and go hungry. The cultural socio-arrangements and leadership ensured that nobody lacked.

Mukami grew up surrounded by many relatives, cousins, and aunts. When one crossed the valley, they would meet more family and friends. Everybody knew everybody, and that's probably why there were greater social responsibilities than today. So, while the chief may have had more goats than others, the chief was also responsible for ensuring nobody was hungry.

Her little recollection of money as a child was how deep her mother's pockets were. Women had ingenious ways of keeping the little money they had safe. Her mother stashed any money she earned in the pockets of her undergarment called Irinda, which was worn under the dress educated women wore to match the dress code imposed by the European Christian missionaries who had brought religion to Kenya. On the other hand, her grandmother kept her money in a Cuka - an item of clothing in a sheet form that almost every Kikuyu woman donned. Typically tied around one's waist as an overskirt, around hair as a headpiece, or wrapped around one's back for carrying a baby while doing chores, gardening, etc. Mukami's grandmother used to tie her coins in one of these Cukas. She would line a coin in the Cuka, tie a knot around it, and do the same with the following coin until she had the whole sheet in knotted coins. Then, she would tie the knotted Cuka around her waist. Not so much for safety but to avoid the coins falling and disappearing.

The next time she learned about money and safety, Mukami was much older, in high school, when they had to pay school fees. Mom would sew their fees into their clothes because they had to travel to school, and that was

Mukami: There's power in Harambee

Mukami was born in Kenya to the Kikuyu people, whose ancestral home is on the slopes of Mount Kenya. Her earliest recollection has nothing to do with money, perhaps due to the absence of it. Wealth was not always counted in currency, and they didn't have a lot of cash transactions growing up. Social Capital was the currency, at least the one that mattered. So, if houses were being built, women worked together and built one family's home. Then, when that was built, they all moved on to the next family's house. If the ladies spent the day digging one garden, they would dig the next person's garden the next day. It was a barter system, and paying cash for labour was alien. There was a communal notion that nobody should

How to Break the Habit

Think in pounds: Planning your budget in pounds helps you understand local prices.

Learn the local cost of living: Learn the average price of rent, food and travel in pounds to help you budget better.

Set goals in pounds: Save for your goals in pounds. This will focus your financial planning on your life in the UK.

Embracing pounds can help you align yourself with the UK's economic situation and give you a sense of belonging and stability sooner. It can change your mindset from an outsider to an integral part of your new community.

PS: Remember to be patient with yourself. It takes time to adapt to a new financial system. You can become familiar with the nuances of the British pound without pressuring yourself to get everything right immediately.

Practical example: Imagine you use a forward contract to lock in an exchange rate of 1.3 for transferring £1,000 to your home currency in six months. Whether the pound weakens or strengthens in that time, you will have locked in a rate that ensures your family will receive the expected amount; this would provide financial predictability and peace of mind, allowing you to focus on other aspects of settling into life in the UK.

Remember that while forward contracts can be a powerful tool for managing currency risk, they come with risks and costs. It's essential to proceed with a clear understanding and cautious approach, ideally with the guidance of a financial adviser or experienced broker. Always check that the Financial Conduct Authority regulates any financial institution you deal with.

Avoid conversion confusion

A common pitfall for newcomers is to convert UK prices into their home currency constantly. This habit makes it challenging to understand the actual cost of living. It can lead to financial mistakes and a slow transition, as constant currency conversion can be a barrier to understanding the exact value of money in your new country. UK prices and living costs are based on sterling and reflect local economic conditions. By constantly comparing these to your home currency, you're not fully engaging with the financial reality around you. This habit can distort your perception of affordability and value, potentially leading to financial mistakes.

Learning Moment: Foreign Exchange

Moving to the UK means learning about exchange rates. Think of it as learning a new language to help you manage your money wisely in your new home. Exchange rates show how much one country's currency is worth in another. They change for various reasons and play a big role in your financial life abroad.

Why exchange rates are important to you:

Sending money home: If you plan to support your family back home, the exchange rate will affect how much money arrives at the other end. A good rate means more value for your hard-earned pounds, so researching and timing your transactions is essential.

Savings and investments: If you're looking to save or invest in the UK or back home, changes in the exchange rate can affect the return on your investments. Knowing when to move your money and where to keep it can protect and even grow your wealth across borders.

Tips for managing exchange rates:

Stay informed: Monitor rates through news, banks or apps. Consider and research alternative money service providers. They are sometimes cheaper than traditional banks and can be an excellent alternative for many banking needs.

Protect your investments: Consider financial strategies such as forward contracts to lock in exchange rates for significant future payments and protect against unexpected rate changes.

Rosaline's story is a powerful exploration of the migrant experience, highlighting the challenges of finding one's place in a world that can be both welcoming and indifferent.

Through Rosaline, we learn that wealth is measured in currency, the legacy we build, and the lessons we pass on. Her journey from Sierra Leone to the UK exemplifies the essence of thriving across borders. She adapted, overcame, and ultimately became a true citizen of two worlds.

characterised Rosaline's early years in the UK. It was a time of euphoric highs and educational lows; each experience overlaid with the richness of learning and the challenge of adaptation.

Rosaline's journey to feeling rooted and integrated in the UK took time and was a slow burn, financially and socially.

Despite holding dual British and Sierra Leonean citizenship, she has only begun engaging actively with the UK's political and social fabric in the last decade. She feels this has been heavily influenced by the painful process of becoming a British citizen.

There was all the red tape, from the horrendous mountains of paperwork to the costly financial burden of application fees and numerous tests. As a qualified nurse who contributed to the NHS and dutifully paid her taxes, she often felt like an outsider, working tirelessly to earn a place that felt like hers by right.

Rosaline's challenges to naturalisation were alienating, but they didn't deter her from continuing to work hard and make significant contributions to cancer research - a feat she humbly admits might not have been possible back in Sierra Leone.

However, it was her encounters with fellow migrants, skilled professionals in their homeland now relegated to menial jobs in the UK, that sharpened her perspective on the systemic barriers many face. For example, the plight of a doctor who had become a cleaner out of necessity rather than choice struck a chord with Rosaline. Her empathy for those caught up in the re-qualification system resonates deeply. The exorbitant costs and bureaucratic hurdles in validating foreign qualifications continue haunting her.

At that moment, standing bewildered in front of the ticket agent, Rosaline faced more than just an unexpected financial hiccup; it was the start of a massive journey of adjustment to her new life in the UK. This was about more than currency differences; it was about entering a new world where all the familiar comforts of home suddenly felt far away.

From that moment on, everything was new, from sharing a room with her sister all her life to the novelty of having her own space.

Then, she got a new job and a salary that seemed HUGE when converted to her home currency. She was in awe and felt RICH as she watched her salary exceed her expenses. "Wow," she thought, "more money this month before last month's is finished?" So, she started splashing it out, shopping sprees, fine dining, you name it, she spent it. On one of her calls home, she told her father, "Don't send me any more money; I have a lot of money here. Let me send you some money instead. So, she started sending money to her family as well. Rosaline revelled in the new-found affluence, and the attention and feel-good factor it brought was euphoric.

Despite all this, Rosaline remained unfamiliar with UK banking and the seemingly crazy world of credit cards. The idea of entrusting her hard-earned money to a bank was alien, almost absurd. She clung to the tangible security of holding onto her cash, keeping her salary under her pillow rather than in a bank account. Credit cards were a foreign concept, more peculiar than practical.

This mixture of new-found independence, financial freedom, and reluctance to embrace conventional banking

This routine wasn't just about selling goods but a lesson in responsibility, teamwork, and trust - a practical experience that taught them core values and life skills that would last a lifetime.

As she grew up and finished high school, Rosaline became obsessed with something her teacher had told her: that with her brilliance, if she came to the UK, she would be phenomenal and make a lot of money. So, she set about persuading her parents to send her abroad. In 1969, they relented and paid for her passage from Sierra Leone to Nigeria, where she would board the APAPA, a steel-hulled steamship built by Harland & Wolff in Glasgow in 1914. It was an eight-day voyage - not the most comfortable - but finally, in the summer of 1969, Rosaline arrived ashore at the port of Southampton.

Exhausted but excited, she looked forward to starting a new chapter. Her excitement was soon tempered by her first harsh new financial reality - when the British West African pound she'd grown up with was suddenly worthless. Surprised when the ticket agent refused her money when she tried to pay for her onward journey from Southampton to London, even though it was "pounds", Rosaline was informed that her kind of pounds was no good here and that she would have to exchange her money for the right kind of pounds. It was a moment of stark realisation: the money she had relied on all her life had been reduced to pieces of paper with no value in this foreign land. This was Rosaline's introduction to the complex world of foreign exchange. It underlined that in her new life, she often faced challenges that required quick thinking and flexibility.

perhaps her earliest unspoken lesson in the importance of financial security and the value of hard-earned money.

Rosaline grew up when Sierra Leone's currency was the British West African pound. Her father was well-paid and had a prestigious job earning £36 a month as an accountant for a Swiss company. This placed them in a privileged category. They enjoyed Swiss luxuries, and Dad was able to build them a wonderful home.

Throughout Rosaline's upbringing, her parents instilled in her and her siblings the importance of money, emphasising the value of hard work and frugality. They learned the value of money by helping their mother sell goods to contribute to their school fees. This taught them the importance of collective effort for the family's well-being.

As teenagers, Rosaline and her siblings prepared for their ultimate chore - their mother balancing a calabash on each of their heads, filled with a colourful assortment of items to sell. Like young entrepreneurs, they would set off, transforming their streets into a bustling neighbourhood marketplace. They worked together, and at the end of each day, they pooled the money they'd earned and gave it to their mother, who, as far as they knew, used it to pay their school fees. What she did with the rest was none of their business.

Rosaline's North West Sail

Eighty-five-year-old Rosaline was born in Sierra Leone's beating heart, and she loved it. She remembers her grandmother, a figure of unwavering strength who kept her money safely tucked away in a sack tied around her waist—Kotoko. The kotoko never left her grandmother's waist; it seemed glued there. Only at night, and even then, all the children would be asleep before she took it off. It was a beautiful memory that stayed with Rosaline,

Learning Moment: UK Pay

Martin's experience highlights the importance of adaptability. The budget that worked for him in Uganda needed reevaluation and adjustment in Scotland, a reminder that financial planning is not a one-time task but an ongoing process that requires flexibility and responsiveness to life's changes.

Understanding your pay structure and the story your payslip tells is valuable.

Your pay slip is a record of your hard-earned money. It describes what you have earned and what some of it is deducted for—usually including tax and National Insurance.

In the UK, most working people, including those on a visa, can also get a workplace pension. This is money saved up for when you retire. To get this, you must be between the age of 22 and the age at which you can get the state pension, earn more than the basic amount set by the government each year, and work in the UK. If this describes you, your job must automatically enrol you into a pension scheme, and your employer must also contribute money to your pension savings on your behalf.

The terminology: Your salary, the money you've earned, may be shown as gross pay, which is the total money before any amounts are reduced. Deductions such as tax and national insurance are taken from this. What you are left with is net pay, which is what you get.

would be £5 an hour, he had expected to get £5 an hour, but suddenly, his pay slip had many deductions that he had not accounted for.

This moment marked a profound shift in Martin's mindset. Initial disillusionment with his take-home pay soon gave way to a critical understanding of budgeting. Martin learned to stretch his income to cover his monthly expenses and save to get through the weekend and the next month. This episode, steeped in innocence and complex learning, was Martin's first financial experience.

Martin's story connects with the experiences of other contributors in this book, who also share their versions of cultural shock and financial enlightenment. Imagine the bewilderment of negotiating prices in a supermarket, a common practice in many African countries, only to be met with fixed prices and non-negotiable tags of a now mostly contactless UK supermarket experience.

Or the realisation that credit, an enabling and ensnaring system, is a double-edged sword many have not wielded before making Scotland Home.

budgeting became his lifeline. With his initial £100 dwindling, a realisation dawned upon him; it was quickly apparent that without a job in Scotland, Dad's £100 parting gift would loom not as a bounty but as a countdown to zero. The transition from Martin's arrival to his initiation into the Scottish economy was swift and full of lessons. On landing at Glasgow Airport, a warm hug from his brother was a fleeting comfort before the stark reality of Scotland's cost of living set in.

Taking a bus from the airport to Glasgow, which cost him five pounds, sent shock waves through Martin's financial consciousness. Converting the cost to Ugandan currency shattered Martin's initial optimism about Scotland's affordability. With each transaction, he mentally converted pounds into Ugandan shillings, a habit that underlined the looming challenge of stretching his £100 to meet his needs. Without an income, the spectre of financial instability loomed large.

Martin's stay with his brother was brief, a mere prelude to his next chapter in Paisley, where his college and student accommodation awaited. The rent, a daunting £250 a month, highlighted his predicament: financial strife was inevitable without a job. Pride prevented him from asking for more money from home, a silent acknowledgement of his family's sacrifices to afford his journey.

So, when he secured a job in a local pizzeria at £5 an hour, he was relieved. The simplicity of calculating his potential earnings against a backdrop of 20 hours a week would soon expose his naivety about taxation. When he received his first pay slip, it was a jarring encounter with reality; the figures didn't match his expectations, and he was hit with taxes he hadn't expected. When he was told that his wage

themselves in the lush landscapes and vibrant cultures that make Uganda the true Pearl of Africa. Martin was deeply rooted in his **Ganda** heritage and tradition, which flows as endlessly as the Nile. Hailing from the Kingdom of Buganda, with its lush landscapes and the grandeur of Lake Victoria's shores, it was a cradle of cultural wisdom and ancestral folklore in the bustling markets of Kampala and the fertile grounds surrounding the royal tombs at Kasubi, principles of trade, stewardship, and negotiation were embedded in Martin's upbringing. The value of education was instilled in him, not just to an end but as a lifelong journey. His father had been his first teacher, guiding him through life's lessons and teaching him to see the world not as it was but as it could be, with opportunities hidden like gems waiting to be discovered, which had inspired his decision to come to Scotland. Martin is now the father of two daughters whom he affectionately refers to as his sunshine and happiness. He endeavours to instill financial discipline in them, relying on financial literacy tools to teach them.

Martin's financial education had been mostly theoretical, discussed in classrooms and at home. Yet, in Scotland, breezes of Uganda. The beautiful, cobbled Scottish streets had no familiar sights and sounds of home. Everything was new and different, and Martin found himself a stranger in a country he longed to call home.

The first few weeks were a whirlwind of emotions and challenges. Martin quickly realised that the £100 his father had given him was barely enough to cope with this new life. The exchange rate was the first shocker, followed closely by the high cost of living. Every expense seemed gigantic when translated into the Ugandan currency he'd grown up with.

A quick recalibration was needed to help Martin understand that what felt like a fortune in Uganda was peanuts in this new world. Right from the eye-watering bus fare from Glasgow airport upon his arrival, it was clear that with each pound spent, the value of money—and the importance of managing it wisely—became starkly evident. Connect this with the backdrop of Martin's early years; Martin's life incidentally began in Scotland - he was born in Glasgow, where his parents were living in Easterhouse - the East End of Glasgow. Unfortunately, following ongoing deep issues of racism, when he was four years old, the family relocated back to Uganda and immersed

Martin's Financial Awakening

Our stories begin with an adventurous spirit named Martin, fresh from the academic confines of boarding school in Uganda, who finds himself on a flight to Scotland. Clutching the £100 note from his father, he gets on the plane feeling like he owns the world, unaware of the financial epiphanies awaiting him. This crisp note, a parting gift from his beloved father, represents financial value and a rite of passage into a world where money speaks a different language. But that was soon to fizzle.

Arriving in Scotland was a cold splash of reality. The cold air that greeted him starkly contrasted with the warm community and the valued collaboration of The Living Memory Association Wee Museum and The National Library of Scotland, we sought the support of the Heritage Lottery Fund. Their belief in our mission has enabled us to capture and preserve these powerful stories for future generations. It has been a beautiful journey of discovery and learning, uncovering new depths of understanding and insight as we have conducted in-depth research, produced a limited podcast series - (Check out "The Immigrants Financial Journey Podcast on your preferred podcast station) and the meticulous compilation of narratives, for this book. I have realised that if we could only dare to listen, attempt to observe, and open our hearts to empathise, we would learn something in every interaction we ever have. This book has been brought together by a village. It truly is the fruit of collective labour, nurtured and harvested by a community in the truest sense. I leave you with this thought:

When people from far and wide migrate to the continent of Africa, they are referred to as expats. When Africans migrate to other parts of the world, they are immigrants. Truer words have never been illustrated than in the African Proverb,

"Until the lion tells the story, the hunter will always be the hero."

It is a great privilege and honour to be a lion and tell the stories of lions. I sincerely thank everyone who has entrusted me with their stories, heritage, and financial journeys. We have reclaimed the narrative, honouring our shared heritages with every word in this book.

With love, Tynah Matembe

Preface

Before I turned the first page of this journey, my life had already been deeply coloured by my move to Scotland sixteen years ago. This move shaped my identity and career as a financial inclusion expert and money coach. The initial challenges of integrating blossomed into lived experiences that illuminated my path and continue to guide my work—positioning me as a natural fit to write this work. I am privileged to author this book as an integral part of the 'An Immigrant's Financial Journey' project led by the Enkula Wellness Hub. This innovative project was born from the team's discovery of a significant gap in the literature on the rich heritage and financial stories of people who have chosen Scotland as their new home. Recognising the importance of sharing these migration experiences, and with the invaluable support of our

African Proverb

"Until the lion tells the story, the hunter will always be the hero."

Chinua Achebe

Table of Contents

African Proverb 3

Preface 4

Martin's Financial Awakening 6

    Learning Moment: UK Pay 11

Rosaline's North West Sail 12

    Learning Moment: Foreign Exchange 18

Mukami: There's power in Harambee 20

    Learning Moment: Navigating the UK Banking System 29

Shupikai: A tale of three currencies 31

    Learning Moment: Leveraging Money Clubs 35

Justin: Hard Work Pays 40

    Learning Moment: Available Financial Support 46

Ife & Ngo: Chop one, Chop two 48

    Learning Moment: The Side Hustle is possible; start a business 55

Kamel: Completely Successfully Blessed 59

    Learning Moment: Positioning Yourself for Career Success . 65

Amiina & Mariama: Smiling Coast of Africa 67

    Learning Moment: Financial Strategies for Raising a Child .. 73

Chapter 9: Eva: Strength of a Woman 76

    Learning Moment: Investing 82

David Going the Mile - Mafuta Minji 85

    Learning Moment: Leaving a Legacy 90

Acknowledgements 92

    A message from the book's illustrator 96

    Project Contributors 98

Thriving Beyond Borders

Managing Money in A New Country